MINISTERS FOR THE 1980s

Ministers for the 1980s

JOHN R. GRAY
ROBERT A. JONES
HERBERT A. KERRIGAN
LESSLIE NEWBIGIN
JAMES PHILIP
GEORGE T. H. REID
COLIN SINCLAIR
JOCK STEIN
DAVID W. TORRANCE
DAVID F. WRIGHT
GEORGE YULE

Edited by

JOCK STEIN

The Handsel Press

1979

Published by
The Handsel Press Ltd.
33 Montgomery Street, Edinburgh

Paperback ISBN 0 905312 09 0

First published 1979

Printed in Great Britain by
Lindsay & Co. Ltd., Edinburgh

Contents

Acknowledgements

The Editor and the Publishers are most grateful to the following for permission to reproduce copyright material: Hodder & Stoughton Ltd for the passage from *Power of Prayer* by Dora Greenwell and P. J. Forsyth, Lutterworth Press for the extract from *Preaching and Congregations* by Von Allmen, and Orbis Books for the extract from *Against Principalities and Powers*. Chapter 6 is reprinted from an article in *The Churchman* by kind permission.

Introduction

JOCK STEIN

This would appear to be the first book specifically about training for the ordained ministry published in Scotland for a long time. In 1969 a book on education for ministry was published in London, written by a Scottish theological teacher, Steven Mackie, then working in Geneva. The year before that, again in England, the De Bunsen Report on the Training of Anglican Clergy came out, and since then various briefer English studies. In 1975 a consultation at Windsor on "The Educational Role of Theological Colleges and Seminaries" was held, to which a Scottish Divinity professor contributed. No survey has yet been published comparable in depth to the East African study, "Equipping for Ministry", which also appeared in 1969.

In Scotland it has apparently been sufficient for the Committee on Education for the Ministry to report annually to the General Assembly and periodically to publish guidelines for understanding and working the existing system. In 1975 Murdo Ewan Macdonald appealed in "The Call to Communicate" for joint education for clergy and laiety, but took for granted the present University context. The Committee of Forty let loose some comments, and had to pass on.

This book urges the Church of Scotland to reconsider its attitude to training for the ordained ministry. The shortcomings of present practice are explored by various writers, some alternatives are put forward, and perhaps most important of all, we are called together as God's people to reform our ideas on theological education and training in the light of faith in Jesus Christ.

One reason why the Kirk may be ready to consider training for "the ministry" in a fresh light is the current rediscovery of ministry as a function of the whole people of God. Years ago George Macleod thought wistfully of a renewed Church where the ordained minister would be fully engaged in the ministry of Word and Sacrament instead of being a jack of all trades. Today church renewal is indeed focusing attention on the special function of the minister as "the servant of the servants of God". Again, parish readjustment may mean fewer ministers, but it often brings them greater responsibility and so greater need for adequate training and continuing education.

However it would be a delusion to think that the world is waiting eagerly for a book about the Church, and especially about ministers. There are many more immediate concerns! Yet with the present eclipse of devolution, the Church of Scotland with its unique national assembly remains in a key position. The nation still hopes for a lead from the Kirk, even if it is unfashionable to ask for too much in public. The people still expect things from their parish minister, even if they are sometimes disappointed.

So if this is a book addressed to the Church (and in particular to the Church of Scotland) it is not because the writers are unconcerned about the life of the Nation. Nor do we believe that an ideal pattern of training can be worked out irrespective of the changes in thought and in society that have taken place in the last hundred years, and then dropped down from heaven to be the final solution to the Kirk's problems! It is right and proper to listen to the agenda the world sets. But the Lord of the Church has set an agenda of proclamation and service, an agenda acknowledged in the articles of faith of the Church of Scotland. A basic responsibility of God's people in each generation is to formulate a theology of training for ministry, asking the question afresh, "What kind of ministry?", before working out detailed methods of training. This David Torrance, parish minister of Earlston, attempts in chapter 1.

Another reason for seeking fresh light on the subject of training is the growing unrest about what is happening in our Theological Colleges, reflected in articles, editorials and correspondence in Life and Work over the past year. To be fair, some of the criticism is misdirected in that the four Divinity Colleges are following guidelines worked out by the Kirk itself through its Committee on Education for the Ministry. College Chairs are filled on the recommendation of Committees half composed of Church representatives. It is possible that the Church is getting exactly what it asks for!

This book is therefore addressed primarily to the Church of Scotland. If the Faculties of Divinity come in for a bit of stick, it is not implied that the blame is wholly, or even mainly, theirs. After all, a Theological College does not make ministers; it is God who calls, and God who nurtures his servants in the fellowship of his Church; it is the Church which tests and sustains such a call. In chapter 2 James Philip, minister of Holyrood Church in Edinburgh, examines these priorities.

Teaching staff in the College sometimes make the point another way. "We cannot train you to be ministers", they say, "we can only give you a theological education." Much training is picked up on the job. John R. Gray, minister of Dunblane Cathedral, makes his contribution to this in chapter 3, but goes on to argue that Theological Colleges and the parish have drifted too far apart. Like Steven Mackie he asks that Practical Theology be seen as the focal theological discipline.

The initial stress on ministry as the calling of the whole Church has not been forgotten. In chapter 4 a healthy protest is registered about the clericalisation of the Church by David Wright, elder, lecturer in Church History and convener of the Readers Committee.

So far no reference has been made to denominations other than the Church of Scotland. Many Church members do not realise that our Colleges, especially at Edinburgh and St. Andrews, educate students from many denominations and several countries. At St. Andrews only about a tenth of the Divinity students are candidates for the C. of S. ministry. At Edinburgh, several denominations are represented on the staff, including two Roman Catholics.

True ecumenism, however, is more than mixing staff with different ecclesiastical traditions. It is a working out of the doctrine of the Incarnation of the Son of God. This basis for theological education is traced back to the Reformation in chapter 5 by George Yule, who came to the Chair of Church History at Christ's College, Aberdeen with the unusual experience of teaching in Australia with Anglicans and Jesuits!

We look out further in chapter 6, which is an article by Lesslie Newbigin, former missionary bishop in India. The churches in Africa and South America are growing fast, and the quality of

Christian thought and leadership in Asia is considerable. As world leadership in the Christian Church more and more shifts towards "third world" countries, it is valuable to look at this wider context for training ministers.

In chapter 7 the scene returns to Scotland. Herbert Kerrigan, advocate, church elder and professor, describes how the present system of educating ministers came to be, how it works, and offers some detailed criticism. Then Colin Sinclair, who sandwiched a year in Africa between study at Stirling University and now New College, offers a student's eye view.

George Reid, formerly minister of the Langstane Kirk, Aberdeen, argues the need for a Church College in chapter 9. There is of course a negative argument from caution that in a rapidly changing society, the Kirk should no longer be dependent on the goodwill of the State (which pays her College teaching staff); but a positive case is put forward for a one-year Church College, grounded with some outline statistics provided by Robert Jones, minister of Allan Church, Bannockburn.

The final chapter by the editor attempts to draw together some of the threads of criticism spun by the other writers, and to indicate some changes which could be undertaken in the near future. It is not a fierce tract for the times, but (like the whole book) a mixture of reflection, analysis and application. I am grateful to James Miller of Dumbarton and to many others for their comments on the ideas contained in it.

We are conscious that we have not done all that might be asked. There is very little on futurology, hardly anything on new areas of ministry outwith the parish. We have not considered the radical alternative of a church without ordained ministers at all. We have not included a woman or a Presbytery Clerk among the writers!

The book follows the convention of using "his" in many cases for "his or her". Capitals are often used for emphasis, but without total consistency throughout the book. Occasionally, the content of different chapters has been allowed to overlap, so that the same important points might be put in different contexts. Scripture quotations are from the R.S.V. unless otherwise indicated.

Each writer has made his own contribution, and may not agree with all that is said elsewhere. We differ, for example, on whether the present system of training simply needs to be overhauled, perhaps by a new generation of committee members, or whether the time has come to change the system altogether. But we share in common a recognition that present ministerial formation is being judged by God and found wanting; a belief that faith, theology and the work of the ordained ministry must be integrated; and further, a conviction that the theology of the Christian Church does not find its root in human consciousness, nor in the modern situation, but in God's own revelation of himself in Jesus as really man and really God. We do not regard this as an optional model no longer intelligible to modern men and women. However we are concerned that it should be earthed in Church practice and in the work of Church committees. May God grant that and more.

Jock Stein
The Steeple Church
Dundee

September 1979

1
What kind of ministry
DAVID W. TORRANCE

Some years ago, Professor William Manson said to a group of New College students, of whom I was one, "Answer in one sentence, what is the purpose of the ministry, and what is your task in entering the ministry?" In response to their thoughtful silence, Prof. Manson himself provided the answer: "To fit people for Heaven!"

To students who had experienced something of the trauma of World War 2, his answer was received either with sympathetic understanding or approval. There were no protests such as might have been raised by a later generation of students who had different experiences of life and by students who were not so familiar with Prof. Manson's outlook and theology. There was nothing narrow, nothing unscripturally limited, nothing shallow in his theological outlook. He had an abiding concern to present Christ to his students in all his wholeness. God was present in unending love and compassion on this earth, in the man Christ Jesus, to redeem the world and to set up on this earth, amid all its turmoil, the Kingdom of Heaven. Yet, this Kingdom, which has come in Jesus Christ, and is present wherever Christ is present in the Holy Spirit (and like the leaven in the parable, throws the whole world into ferment) directs our attention forward to a future apocalyptic event when Christ will return as Lord and King in a visible way. The Kingdom of Heaven which has come awaits the final Day when Christ will come and cleanse and renew the heavens and the earth, so that they become the New (or re-newed) Heaven and Earth. Christ came therefore to set up his Kingdom on earth and to call people out of the kingdoms of this world into the Kingdom of Heaven and therefore into the ultimate enjoyment of the New Creation. In that context, Prof. Manson said: "The one purpose of the ministry" (reflecting the Ministry of Christ) "is to fit people for Heaven."

Despite all the limitations, difficulties and dangers from misunderstanding, in seeking to answer such a question in one sentence, his answer is surely correct scripturally! It interprets the direction and emphasis of Christ's Ministry and, therefore, of our ministry when it is in Christ. What follows in this chapter, will be an attempt to develop this answer.

I

The Reformers frequently spoke of the priesthood of the whole Church. What they called "the ministry of Word and Sacrament" was a special ministry, or office, within the ministry of the whole Church. Only when this ordained ministry was fulfilled humbly, faithfully and obediently under God, was the whole Church able to engage in her God-given ministry and to become apostolic, evangelistic, pastoral as the Body of Christ on earth, the Body of which Christ is the Head, and thereby to be the Bride prepared for the Bridegroom at his coming. That is, only as the whole Church, and thereby every member of the Church, engages corporately and together in all the varied forms of God-given, Spirit-empowered ministry, is the Ministry of Christ set forth in wholeness before the world and Christ most openly present and active in love and saving power. No one person and no one section of the Church can exercise the whole ministry of the Church, or reflect in word and deed, in spirit and life, the whole Ministry of Christ; and never alone and apart from the Church, which is the Body of Christ; that ministry belongs to the whole Church and, in part, to the whole congregation in one place.

The ministry of Word and Sacrament, therefore, is a particular ministry commissioned by God to assist in the building up of the Body of Christ in order that the Church may engage through the Spirit in the total Ministry of Christ for the salvation of the world. It is a sad fact, however, as Arnold Bittlinger stresses,[1] that we today have often only one ministry remaining in the Church, that of the pastor! The fact that this is so, and true in Scotland today, means sadly that the Church today is failing to understand, to reflect and to embody the whole Ministry of Jesus Christ in his love and redemption of the world. Consequently the ordained ministry is understood and exercised in too limited a way, either emphasising only one small aspect of Christ's total Ministry, or, even worse, departing from it, no matter in how sincere and well-intentioned a way, along the lines of man's own opinions, or in some form of Christian activism. That is to say, when the ministry of the Church is reduced to only the pastor, then the temptation is open for the minister to present Christ in a limited way (and in the circumstances it is impossible to do otherwise for his understanding and presentation of the Gospel is now fragmented) or for the minister to present his own ideas and opinions in place of God's Word and to seek to forward the cause of Christ by the use of secular, or even political, means.

It is in harmony with Calvin's doctrine of the Royal Priesthood of Christ and of the Church reflecting and exercising that Priesthood through Word and Spirit, in prayer, to say: an ordained minister of Word and Sacrament is called by God to be the leader of an orchestra, and not a one man band! Only the orchestra (the whole Church as she exercises her ministry aright) can echo the praise of Heaven and sound forth the praise of God which is rightly offered by Christ alone.

There is surely urgent need today, therefore, for the Church to consider afresh the doctrine of the ministry of the whole Church and within that, the special office of the ordained ministry. To do that, however, we must first and foremost look at the Ministry of Christ.

II

In considering the Ministry of Jesus Christ, it is important to note the complete harmony and agreement between what Jesus said or taught and what Jesus did; and equally between what he said and did and his own person. What Jesus said and did, he was and is in his own person and being. As such, he is himself the truth and fountain of all truth in word and being. Jesus came talking about the Kingdom and saying, "Repent . . . the Kingdom of God is at hand" (Mark 1:15). Yet, the Kingdom is present wherever Jesus is present; and those who repent and are united to Christ in faith, are within the Kingdom. Jesus reigns over them through his Spirit. In the words of the Sermon on the Mount, Jesus laid on his followers and on his Church a divine obligation, concerning how God commands those within the Kingdom to live. Yet, the Sermon on

the Mount is a description of the very life that Jesus lived. He was
and is the personal embodiment of his teaching. He came
proclaiming God's love for the world; and he himself was the
embodiment of love for the world. In his miracles of forgiving sins,
healing, cleansing and raising the dead, together with his Death
for us sinners on the Cross, we see the enactment and personal
embodiment of God's love and compassion. He came preaching a
Gospel of salvation from sin, death and the powers of darkness. In
his mighty deliverances of people from the power of sin, in his
casting out of evil spirits, in his Death on the Cross and in his
Resurrection, Jesus brought about salvation, reconciliation and
peace between God and man and between man and man, and that
salvation, reconciliation and peace is embodied in his own person.

This he offers freely as a gift to all, and we receive and enjoy it
only as we are united to Christ Jesus who embodies all that he
taught, promised and did. So there is laid on the Church in her
ministry, and on the particular office of the ordained ministry, the
divine obligation of being true to Christ and living out in action
and life, all that the Church proclaims in Christ. That is why the
Church's own standard of life is so important and why the
churches have rightly demanded of the ordained ministry no
compromise in their life style.[2]

The Reformers in speaking of the Ministry of Christ, his Royal
Priesthood and Atonement, spoke of his Incarnation, his Life on
earth, his Death, his Resurrection, his Ascension and his return in
the Spirit at Pentecost. Each stage is important for the
understanding of his mission.

In his Incarnation, we see God coming down into all the chaotic
disorder, weakness, suffering and sin of this world and becoming
man. In becoming man, a creature in the midst of his creation, he
has wonderfully assumed our nature and thereby guaranteed for
all time our creaturely being and the being of all creation. That is
to say, on the one hand, man remains man and will not be
overwhelmed and annihilated in his sin by God's holiness and the
condemnation of his sin. All men continue in life and are for ever
related to Jesus Christ in his Life and also in his Death on their
behalf. As Paul says, because Christ died for all, so all share in his
Death (2 Cor 5:19). Hence, all share in his Resurrection! This does
not mean that all will be saved, or resurrected to life. Sin remains
and mysteriously enters into that relationship which all men have
with the risen Christ, so that, as Jesus taught, there is a twofold

B

resurrection, namely, a resurrection of life and a resurrection of judgment or condemnation (John 5:29). On the other hand, man remains man, and will remain a creature even in the Kingdom of God. He will not become divine.

At the same time, through his Incarnation, Christ has abolished all false distinctions between what is spiritual and what is secular and proclaimed in word, deed and life that he is for ever concerned to cleanse and renew man himself, together with the whole structure of society and the whole order of creation. The temptation of the Church and her ministry to separate the spiritual and material issues of the Gospel, as if one should be held important without the other, is the temptation not to take the Incarnation seriously. As Dr. J.S. Stewart has rightly said, "It is an unholy divorce those Christians are aiding and abetting who separate religion from such material issues as feeding the hungry, rescuing the refugee and enfranchising the racially disinherited".[3]

Perhaps our greatest need today, however, is to seek to understand the contribution of the Life of Christ to his Ministry. This is what the Church throughout her history has so often failed to do, or so it seems. There is no mention of the Life of Christ in the Apostles' and Nicene Creed. There is a remarkable silence concerning it in the Councils of the early Church. Calvin was deeply conscious of it; he linked it in his Institutes with the concepts of "Salvation by grace alone" and "Union with Jesus Christ". Yet the Church, in the years that followed, practically omitted any reference to the Life of Christ, as is clear from the omissions in the Westminster Confession of Faith and in the Longer and Shorter Catechisms. In more recent years there have been many attempts to seek to recover the Jesus of history. Many of these, however, in so far as they have not been based on the primary confession of Jesus Christ as at once God and man, and have not been efforts to understand the Life of Jesus within the context of his total mission reaching from his Incarnation to Pentecost and his Return to this earth at the last, have sadly failed to represent the Christ of the Gospel story. There is, however, great need for the Church to try and understand the contribution to his Ministry of Jesus' Life. For it is the kind of person Jesus was, the kind of life he lived, the acts which he performed and the way in which he performed them, together with all that he said and taught, which give content and shape to what our ministry in him, and in union with him, should be.[4] It is the inner life of Jesus Christ lived in union with the Father, his life incarnating the love of God among men, which gives to our ministry in his name, and to the ministry of the Church, its inner form and life. So Paul prays for the Churches to whom he ministered and to the Church in Galatia, "I am again in travail until Christ" (Christ in all his fullness) "be formed in you".

When we look at the Life of Christ, as an integral part of his mission to the world, we see each of his mighty miracles of forgiving sins, healing, cleansing, casting out evil spirits and raising the dead, as signs pointing to the glorious presence of God at work in the world. In each miracle, the veil is momentarily drawn aside and we see God present in the Man Jesus, on our behalf, overcoming suffering and evil, conquering and casting out the powers of darkness — a foretaste of the triumph and victory of Jesus' Resurrection and Ascension to reign over all, that he might give to his people the new life of the Kingdom.

In Jesus Christ, we see God coming not in condemnation of man in his rebellion and sin but in love and compassion drawing alongside of man, identifying himself with man in his weakness and alienation from God; and wondrously taking on himself the burden, the responsibility and the guilt of man's sin and taking on himself his own divine condemnation, so that man, through this wonderful exchange that God has effected with him may henceforth go free by grace and through faith in Christ, and be clothed with Christ's purity and righteousness, and be equipped with Jesus' own life, conferred as a gift of grace. In Jesus' Life, we have a foretaste of what he accomplished in his Death and Resurrection.

In the man Jesus, God worked out for us and on our behalf, a true human response to God's offer of grace and salvation. Jesus, on our behalf, offered to God, in his coming to earth, in his Life and Death, a perfect human obedience. By his perfect obedience, he fulfilled all the promises of God whereby the one who so obeys God will live for ever and be truly blessed. Therefore, once our sins have been atoned for, our guilt cancelled, our condemnation removed, the risen Lord offers us by grace his own human life of obedience to the Father, lived out on our behalf, so that in him we may look up and call him "our Father", and know that in Christ we belong to one family.

Once we consider the Life of Christ as an integral part of his mission to the world, then we need to take a fresh long look at

Pentecost and the Acts of the Apostles, where we see the same person of Jesus, now risen and alive, at work in his Church through his Spirit: and we need to reconsider Paul's doctrine of union with Christ.[5] Here we can be grateful to many recent writers within the Renewal Movement, such as Tom Smail, Colin Urquhart, T.S. Bennet, A. Bittlinger, Canon Glennon, Father MacNutt and Cardinal Suenens, who linking the Life of Christ with the Holy Spirit at Pentecost have given us fresh insights into the manifold gifts and ministries, which Christ has given to the Church and in which ordained ministers share with others.

Again, once we consider the Life of Jesus as integral to his mission to the world, then the Church must seek not only to witness to God as he comes to us in saving grace but also to witness to him as he takes our part; for Jesus stands solidly alongside of us, as we and our fellow sinners approach the Father, in Jesus, and along with Jesus. That means that the Church in her ministry must learn in love and compassion, through the Spirit and in prayer, to identify herself with those outside the Kingdom, so that we, along with them, and together with Jesus, may approach the Father and together enter the life of grace. It also means that the Church and the ordained ministry must learn in a new way to exercise "vicarious faith" and "vicarious prayer", so that standing alongside those who are outside the Kingdom, we might exercise faith and prayer on their behalf to claim for them, in a way in which they cannot at present do, the promises and blessings of God in Christ.[6] In this way, in Christ, through the Holy Spirit, and in prayer, we seek to witness to and embody the Ministry of Jesus, when he offered on our behalf a human response to God's grace.

III

The Death of Christ is the climax of his coming. The angel anticipated it in announcing his Birth (Matt 1:21). Jesus affirmed it: "What shall I say, Father, save me from this hour? No, for this purpose I have come to this hour" (John 12:27), and again, "I came to cast fire upon the earth, and would that it were already kindled! I have a baptism to be baptised with, and how I am constrained until it is accomplished" (Luke 12:49, 50; also John 10; 10-18; Acts 2:23, etc.). Moreover the Gospels are written in such a way as to focus attention, not primarily on his birth, nor on his teaching and mighty works, but on his suffering, death and resurrection. Any attempt to portray the Ministry of Jesus, which fails to focus attention on his Death and Resurrection, is not true to the witness of Scripture. Likewise the ministry of the Church and the ordained ministry, unless it takes the Death and Resurrection as central to all that is said and done, is sadly failing to be true to Christ and his Ministry and is correspondingly ineffective.

In Jesus, God took on himself all the suffering and sin of the world. He assumed responsibility for our guilt and alienation from God and at the point where man was furthest from God in sin and rebellion, there he made reconciliation and peace, even through Jesus' atoning Life and Death. In Jesus' Resurrection and Ascension, he triumphed over all and, as a gift of grace, offers life and peace to all. Finally he will come, and in virtue of Jesus' atoning Life, Death and Resurrection, will cleanse and renew all creation. Everything that had gone before, the mighty acts of God's redemption witnessed to by the prophets, was a preparation for what he came and did and will yet do in Jesus Christ. All that he had hitherto done in and through Jesus' birth, teaching and mighty miracles, was a foretaste and preparation for this supreme event of reconciliation, wrought out finally through his Death and Resurrection and now made possible for us in union with Jesus through faith. Here is grace and love divine where sin is dealt with at its heart and man is offered eternal deliverance and the joy of the Kingdom of Heaven!

In the parable of the strong man (Matt 12:29ff, and Luke 11:21ff), Jesus anticipated what he was about to do at the Cross, where sin or satan, this personal demonic power, would be overthrown and bound, so that the kingdom of this world, which he had usurped, might be plundered by God, and men and women set free in Christ Jesus. Christ's Death has the dimension of an unseen battle between Christ and the demonic powers of darkness, which have usurped control of this world and seized control of men and nations. Now they would be, and were, overthrown (John 12:31; Luke 10:10). "It was his Death that was satan's final doom", wrote P.T. Forsyth.[7] "The wickedness of the world is after all a bull in a net, a chained beast kicking itself to death." This wickedness, this satanic power is still alive and is still able to hurt and destroy those who come too near, yet its power is limited and largely controlled. It has been caught in a net and bound by Christ.[8] As such the Church must courageously, triumphantly proclaim the victory of Christ and that his victory is for all who would receive him and be united to him in faith. Christ has conquered all satanic powers. What then of the last enemy — death? "Men still have to die; yet in the Cross and Resurrection of Jesus, death — this most omnipotent of the principalities and powers — has finally been conquered; so that of those who are united with Christ and his victory it is true to say that they have passed out of death into life."[9]

The Resurrection is the supreme unveiling of God in Jesus Christ triumphing over sin, death and the powers of darkness and hell. The Resurrection puts the divine seal on Jesus' coming to earth and on all that Jesus said and did throughout his earthly ministry. It seals the fact that God and the world are reconciled for ever and that in Christ, God is altogether turned to the world in redeeming love. The Resurrection was no mere providential afterthought, no addendum to God's scheme of salvation. It belongs to the very heart of God's salvation of the world. Without the Resurrection, all the events that went before would be robbed of their saving force. In themselves they are powerless to save. As Paul says, "if Christ be not risen", our faith, our hope, our preaching are all in vain, for there is no deliverance and no salvation (I Cor 15:12ff). Praise God, however, Christ is risen! And with his Resurrection everything that God has ever done in Jesus comes alive and is stamped with divine meaning and purpose, to this end that man and the world might be saved to God.[10]

The glorious news of the Resurrection, however, is not simply, as some have narrowly imagined, the glad news that there is a glorious life beyond the grave. It is that, but it is far more. God in Jesus Christ has broken triumphantly into this world of ours. He has wrought out his mighty victory over sin and death and over all the uncoordinated, indeterminate mass of suffering, which goes far beyond man's sin and rebellion against God. He has triumphed victoriously over all the powers of darkness and hell, and man is called to share today in that victory of Christ. This is the Gospel, the Good News, which the Church is called to proclaim: and what glorious things happen when the Church does so!

Jesus Christ rose from the dead and ascended to reign. All power in heaven and earth is now in his hand. He who bore our sin and guilt and reconciled us to God, now reigns.[11] Reigning he watches over the Church, guides her, preserves her, builds her up to his glory and at the same time watches over and directs the course of all men and nations, overruling the wrath and wickedness of men and making all things work together for the accomplishment of his purposes of final redemption and renewal. In his Ascension, he continues to exercise with divine power his Ministry to men (Heb 1:3, 8:1, etc.). This too belongs to the very heart of the Good News which the Church is called to proclaim to the world. "And so, beside the principle, 'He died for our sins according to the Scriptures', rises the other complementary principle, 'He sitteth at the right hand of God in the glory of the Father'. On these foundations, everything else is built."[12]

Ascended, he is yet present in his Church through the Holy Spirit, powerfully present, in redeeming love and power, pleading the merits of his Death and Resurrection to the Father and recommissioning his Church ever anew, to go forth in his mission to the world. If there is great need today to understand afresh the positive contribution of the Life of Jesus to his whole Ministry to the world, there is likewise need to understand afresh the Ministry and mission of the risen, ascended and victorious Lord present in his Church today through the Holy Spirit, working out and seeking to work out great miracles of grace and salvation, of which we have a vivid foretaste in the Gospel narratives. Here again, we can be grateful to many writers in the Renewal Movement who have been helping the Church to understand afresh the presence and power of the Holy Spirit and to understand that God in Christ is alive today and actively at work in the Church and in the world. The remarkable advance of certain Churches throughout the world today (e.g. in South America, Kenya and Indonesia), is clearly due in part to a new realisation of the presence and power of the Holy Spirit.

The risen, victorious Christ is alive and at work in and through his Church today, calling men and women out of darkness and bondage to sin and death, into light and freedom and life: calling them gladly to accept his offered gift of salvation and new life in the Kingdom of Heaven. This he continues to do, until as the Apostles' Creed says, "He shall come to judge the quick and the dead". Christ has come to this world in redeeming love and power. He is here today and we look forward in anticipation to his final Coming at the end of time, when as true King and Judge, he will come to cleanse and renew this world which he has created and redeemed and thereby transform all things so that they become the new Heaven and Earth, in which he will cause his people, then made perfect, to dwell with him, seeing him face to face. Christ's Ministry points forward in expectation of the final Day when his saving mission will be fulfilled. Likewise the Church ministers under Christ, in the power of the Holy Spirit, with her eyes on that final Day and prays: "Even so come, Lord Jesus".

Such is the Ministry of Christ Jesus which he lays on his Church, which is his Body and of which he is the Head. Such is the Ministry which he calls his Church to reflect and embody in word and act and prayer, in the power of the Holy Spirit.

IV

How then can we witness to, and embody in the Spirit, the Ministry of Christ in all its wealth and fulness, as he summons men and women out of the kingdoms of this world into the joyous new life of the Kingdom of Heaven, in anticipation of that day when he will rejoice with his people and they with him in the new Creation? We can do so in the first instance, by seeking to keep constantly before us in prayer, the whole Ministry of Christ in all its facets and wealth: and secondly, by seeking to encourage the whole Church to fulfil her ministry, in humble acknowledgment that only the whole Church acting together in the Spirit, can begin to represent the Ministry of Christ in wholeness. As mentioned earlier, when the Church becomes reduced in her ministry to the pastor only, then her understanding of Christ's Ministry is limited, and consequently her own ministry, and the ministry of Word and Sacrament, is impoverished.

What is required of those who are called to the ordained ministry?

Barth answers this question in a most challenging way.[13] The ministry calls for complete sincerity and faith in Christ Jesus, complete dedication in prayer, complete dedication of mind and intellect in order to wrestle with and to seek to understand and interpret for this day and age, what God is saying through his Word. It requires discipline of body and great sensitivity of spirit to the joys and sorrows of people around. It requires great love and compassion for everyone and great courage, and readiness to give oneself, and to go on giving, as Christ did, to the uttermost. The pastor must be conversant with the thinking, with the outlook, with the aspirations, of people of all walks of life from all backgrounds: able to speak and act with great naturalness and yet ever ready, at all times, to represent Christ and to confront men and society with Christ's summons to salvation. A heavy task! Indeed the heaviest of all tasks!

What is required in the actual exercise of the ministry? The following are some basic requirements.

Salvation by Grace Alone.   As ministers of Word and Sacrament it is essential that we ourselves have experienced the forgiveness of God and have received that salvation which is a gift of God's grace. We ourselves must have a deep personal awareness that neither we nor anyone deserve the salvation of God. Nothing that anyone of us can do will merit it. It is not a reward of good works. It is not even a reward of faith. It is a gift which we receive only by the mercy and kindness of God, a gift of God's grace which we receive through faith. Not only so! We only truly continue in the ministry, in the right way, as we ourselves share ever more deeply in that experience of grace and forgiveness. For only so can we helpfully minister to the spiritual needs of our people, draw alongside them, identify ourselves with them and help them, with us, and in company with Christ Jesus, to come to the Father and share in that salvation which is by grace alone.

Union with Jesus Christ.   Another basic requirement throughout our ministry is our continual union, through Word and Spirit, with Jesus Christ, who comes to us clothed in his Life, Death and Resurrection (Calvin). Only if we ourselves know what it means to die with Christ to ourselves, our sins and the world, and to rise with Christ to new life and to the service of the Kingdom of Heaven, can we help others to be united with Christ in his Life, Death and Resurrection, either in worship at home or in church, or to enjoy that intimacy of communion with the incarnate, crucified and risen Christ which is made possible as we pray, meditate on Scripture, and share in the Lord's Supper.

Only if we rejoice in union with Christ and know the triumph and victory of his Resurrection, can we helpfully encourage others to that enjoyment.

The Holy Spirit.   A further basic requirement is our dependence on the Holy Spirit. The ministry of the Word of God is begun, directed, ordered and achieved by Christ Jesus.[14] It is therefore from first to last a work of the Holy Spirit, and by the Holy Spirit, for Christ's glory. It is so easy once a person knows that he is commissioned by Christ, to press on and to seek to pursue his ministry in his own strength, in accord with his own ideas and opinions, which however good and religiously well intended, are nonetheless still only man's ideas. This however is not the ministry to which Christ calls us. Christ is at all times the Head, the sole Authority, and the Church, of which the minister is but part, is his Body. Only when a minister is consciously dependent on the Holy Spirit, asks for the Holy Spirit (Luke 11:13) and is continually filled and possessed by the Holy Spirit, can he rightly exercise his ministry in the power of Christ. Only then can he say with Paul, in whatever situation he is in, "I live, yet not I, but Christ lives in me" (Gal 2:20).

The Word of God.   A minister must have a deep personal knowledge of the Word of God. Like Joshua in his keeping of the Law (Josh 1:8), he must read it and meditate on it day and night, so that it penetrates the warp and woof of his being, controls his mind, directs his attitude and influences his whole way of life. His ear must ever be open and his mind and soul attentive to hear what God is saying to him and to the Church. He has the special task of making the Word of God known and of helping the Church to listen to the voice of God. He must take every opportunity in public worship, in the homes of his people and elsewhere, to encourage his people in the daily, prayerful, reading of the Bible, so that they may live in constant communion with the living Lord.

Prayer.   "Prayer is a grace, a gift from God."[15] A minister needs to have shared and to go on sharing ever more deeply in this grace, if he would teach his people to pray and his ministry would be effective in Christ. He must be at all times a person of prayer, his life nourished and moulded by the Word of God.

Prayer is union and communion with Jesus Christ in the presence of the Father. "No one prays", wrote Dora Greenwell, "who does not pray in the freedom of Christ's life, and work and death . . . The measure of faith in his merits and sacrifice, will be found to be the measure of prayer in the case of any individual or any church . . . It is the sight of the Cross, and of all the tremendous associations that are bound up with it — the sense of guilt, of condemnation, of deliverance, of infinite loss, and everlasting gain — that brings, that binds the soul to prayer. It is this sight that makes of every awakened soul a priest, an intercessor, no longer bringing, as does the mere nominal believer, his fruit of the lips . . . but joining its every petition to the might of that prevailing blood, which is itself the most powerful of all intercessions."[16]

Prayer is based on the certainty that God hears and answers prayer. Prayer is grounded on that assurance (Calvin). In true prayer, we never pray alone. We pray in company with Jesus, for "Jesus Christ bids us pray with him and in him".[17] "Calvin goes so far as to say that we pray through his mouth. Jesus Christ speaks by virtue of what he has been and what he has suffered in obedience and faithfulness to his Father; and we pray as it were through his mouth inasmuch as he enables us to draw near and be heard, and he intercedes for us."[18]

Prayer in Jesus Christ is insistent in its intercession. It is claiming all that God has promised in grace and it is praying with a God-given determination, with thanksgiving, until we, and the Church for whom we pray, see the answer. Every minister needs to learn to pray like Jacob as he wrestles with the Lord at Penuel, or like Abraham as he pleads with God for Sodom, or like Moses as he stands in the breach "interceding for Israel and asking God to blot out his name out of the book of life, if that were needful to save Israel",[19] or like our Lord praying with great agony in Gethsemane as he receives the peace and power from the Father, to go forth and accomplish the salvation of the world.

Prayer is guided, inspired, controlled by the Word of God. It is holding up to God what he himself has said, and promised, for his own glory. It is seeing what he has promised as it relates to the present situation which confronts us: and it is claiming with thanksgiving and assurance the fulfilment of that promise. Only when we pray, in this way, are we praying in accord with God's will, praying together with Jesus, praying in the Spirit. This means that as ministers, we need to be deeply conversant with the promises of God, to live and move in their atmosphere and to be able in prayer, to relate these promises to everyday life.

Prayer is permeated through and through with thanksgiving and praise to God. Thanksgiving and praise should form the major part of prayer, as they are the major part of faith. The minister is, and must be, essentially a thankful person, deeply conscious of, and deeply grateful for, all that God in his mercy has done in Jesus Christ and continuously grateful for all that God is doing today. He must be able to rejoice and give thanks to God in all circumstances (I Thes 5:18) and at all times and for everything (Eph 5:20; Col 3:17; Phil 4:4-7). Only in this way can he encourage, inspire and lead his people to praise God.

Prayer, for the minister of the Gospel, must be such that he can pray naturally and at ease in public worship and, equally, in the homes of his people, with the elderly and equally with the very young, at the bedside of the sick and dying, and also, when occasion requires, or proves helpful, when he meets his people in the open air, or in their place of work. If our people would learn to pray and to relate prayer to everyday life and affairs, surely it is a matter of supreme importance that we in the ministry can, and should, encourage them, and set for them the example of doing this along with them.

The Representative of Christ.   It is basic to the ministry that we see ourselves, and the Church, as ambassadors, or personal representatives, of Christ. We often shrink from this side of the ministry: yet, scripturally, it is the case. As Jesus called the Apostles so he calls us today, into close communion with himself, to hear what he has to say, to see what he is doing, to walk with him, to be one with him in the Spirit, in such a way that the risen Christ works in us, and in the Church, doing today even greater works than he did during his earthly Ministry (John 14:12).

When as representatives of Christ, we act in prayer, and in obedience to his Word, and in the Spirit, Christ comes as he has promised, and confronts men and women in grace and saving power. He comes to them as we preach the Word, as we administer the Sacraments, and as we witness to him, and speak of him, from day to day, in the homes of our people and elsewhere. As ministers we are given a great privilege and entrusted with a great responsibility.

The ordained ministry, then, is a call from God the Father to witness to Christ who is alive today and is calling all men to be saved. In this context, it is indeed, as Professor Manson put it, the call from God to seek under his grace, "to fit people for Heaven".

NOTES

1. Arnold Bittlinger, *Gifts and Ministries* p.91
2. Bittlinger, *ibid.* p.98
3. J.S. Stewart, *A Faith to Proclaim* p.18
4. Stewart, following Deissman, notes in *A Man in Christ* p.155 that the words "in Christ", or some cognate expression such as "in the Lord", "in him", occur 164 times in Paul, but never in the Synoptics.
5. Stewart, *A Man in Christ* p.147
6. Jim Glennon, *Your Healing is within you* p.116 ff.
7. P.T. Forsyth, *The Glorious Gospel* pp.6-7
8. O. Cullman, *Christ and Time* p.198

 9. Stewart, *A Faith to Proclaim* p.97
10. K. Barth, *Credo* p.108
11. Barth, *Ibid.* p.107
12. W. Manson, *Jesus and the Christian* p.131
13. Barth, *God in Action* p.58 ff.
14. Barth, *ibid.* p.73
15. Barth, *Prayer and Preaching* p.16
16. D. Greenwell, *The Power of Prayer* p.151 f.
17. Barth, *Prayer and Preaching* p.31
18. Barth, *ibid.* p.17
19. Forsyth, *The Power of Prayer* p.134

2
The call to the ministry

JAMES PHILIP

The call to the ordained ministry has its origin in God. It is a divine institution and activity, as the New Testament is at pains to point out, often by implication[1], and as often explicitly (cf Heb 5:4; Gal 1:12-16; Eph 3:8). A minister is not self-appointed to his task: he is called to it by God, and it is this alone that authorises and authenticates his ministry. "One cannot set oneself up as a minister of God. If we have the right and hence the duty to preach, it is neither our faith, nor our learning, nor our ambition, nor our love for our fellow-men which gives it to us: it is God. This is another way of saying that God remains master of his Word, that it is not at our disposal."[2]

I

Our starting point, therefore, for a true understanding of Christian ministry must be the New Testament teaching on the subject. A cardinal passage is Paul's statement in Ephesians 4:7-16, in which he unfolds the picture of an ascended and victorious Lord on the initiative to bless his people, leading captivity captive, and giving gifts to men. Among the gifts he gives are those of ministry, for the perfecting of the saints and the edifying of the body of Christ. It is an impressive and wonderful picture, and it has a number of important implications. One is that when the ascended Lord is at work in his Church, and when he is given his place as the Church's rightful Lord, then there is the distribution of his gifts to the Church — gifts not only of ministry (although this is our particular concern) but also other things — helpers, administrators, leaders (cf 1 Cor 12, Rom 12) — everything in fact that makes up the many-sided working of a living fellowship, with its enormously rich variety of expression.

Paul is of course speaking of the institution of the New Testament Church in Acts: "He ascended up on high . . . and gave gifts to men." But as he gave, so he gives. This is the continuing pattern. And we may say assuredly that where he is allowed to be the living Lord of the Church, there he gives the gifts of ministry to his people. In such a context we should expect him to call men to the work of the ministry. Indeed, where there is a living Church, Christ does call men to the work of the ministry.

By the same token, the converse may also be asserted. The Church is not always a living Church: sometimes it grows cold, losing its first love, becoming complacent, worldly, unfaithful, even apostate. When this happens, Christ is edged out of his rightful place, and grieved out of the Church that he bought with his own blood. That this is a solemn possibility is borne out by the picture given in Rev 3:20 of Christ standing outside the door of the Church.

It is when the Church is like this, cold, barren and unfaithful, that the gifts are withheld, and true life grinds to a standstill, and lesser expedients take over — professionalism comes in, and substitute categories do duty for the true gifts of ministry that Christ always intended should be exercised among his people.

This could be put another way: when the Church is dead, or in a state of spiritual decay, the call to the ministry is not heard and responded to. It was when the prophet Isaiah saw the Lord high and lifted up, and in that revelation came to a renewed experience of forgiveness and cleansing, that he heard the voice of God saying: "Whom shall I send, and who will go for us?" There are times when men are not near enough to God to hear the call to service. They are simply not within earshot of the divine voice.

This explains why, when the Church is revived and renewed, candidates for the holy ministry begin to appear in increasing numbers. It is the coming of the ascended Lord into the midst once again, bestowing his gifts upon his people. It is certainly not by accident, for example, that the evangelical awakening of the mid-19th century in Britain led directly to an increase in personnel in one year of twenty-five per cent on the mission fields of the world. It would be an instructive and valuable piece of research to examine the relation between the numbers of candidates for the ministry in the past twenty-five years and the nature and quality of the ministries that have produced them. Perhaps there is a greater need for an assessment of this nature than has hitherto been appreciated: perhaps, too, this is one of the ways in which we might hear what the Spirit is saying to the churches in our day.

It may seem an extreme, even harsh and censorious, judgment to make to speak of the Church as being in a Laodicean state, and to impute the growing manpower crisis in the ministry to spiritual malaise at its heart; but it may be that facing such an unpalatable truth in all honesty and penitence is a necessary preliminary to any hope of renewal.

It is true, of course, that a revived Church and a biblical ministry are themselves the gift of Christ to his people, and that in sovereign grace he sometimes bestows the inestimable gift of a prophetic ministry in a time of barrenness and deadness, which eventually leads to a reviving of the Church, and a renewing of the gifts of ministry. But even in the context of that sovereign gift being bestowed, it is still true to say that prayer may well have lain behind the giving. This is why the great burden, in face of the need of the Church, must always be: "Pray therefore the Lord of the harvest to send forth labourers into his harvest" (Luke 10:2). Here, again, is a truer index than is generally supposed of the vitality or otherwise of the Church. The history of mid-nineteenth century Scotland shows that, prior to the great evangelical awakening then, one in every four of the communicant members of the United Presbyterian Church was attending its regular prayer meetings.[3]

II

In the context, then, of a living Church, in which the ascended Lord bestows gifts of ministry, how does that bestowal express itself? How does the call come, and how is it recognized?

The Scriptures emphasise several different characteristics of a true call. First of all, it is spoken of in terms of an inner constraint. Paul's statement in 1 Cor 9:16 is very emphatic: "Necessity is laid upon me. Woe to me if I do not preach the gospel."[4] In Philippians 3:12 he speaks of being "apprehended of Christ Jesus" (KJV); this is particularly true of his calling as an apostle, but it is just as true for any ministry of the Word. The call, then, is an inner constraint in a man's spirit, summoning him to the divine service.

That inner constraint can come relatively suddenly, or it can come gradually, even imperceptibly. But come it must: it is always there in a true call of God. Moreover, what requires to be stressed in this connection is its inevitability. A man is hedged in, even hemmed in, and cornered, until he sees that there is no option for him. He can do no other.

In this connection two points may be made: first of all, it has been said with a good deal of truth that if a man feels able to follow anything else as a career it is fairly certain that he is not called to the ministry. If the ministry is only one of a number of live options, it is not for him. On the other hand, if for him the obvious and inevitable form of Christian commitment and consecration for service is preaching, then this is strong *prima facie* evidence of a genuine call.

The idea of inner constraint by itself has, of course, its very real dangers, as the history of the Church has often proved, and there is a need for some objective criteria by which it can be confirmed and validated. We are to "try the spirits" whether they be of God. This is a very necessary exercise in the matter of guidance in general, and particularly relevant so far as a call to the ministry is concerned.

Two considerations are important here. Firstly, the spiritual judgment of other mature and discerning Christians should be sought, considered and listened to. It is often through the wise and spiritually objective discernment of others that we are enabled to try the spirits. The doctrine of providence plays a part in this. God ordinarily equips men in advance with enduements for service by bestowing aptitudes and capabilities. Paul was separated unto God from his mother's womb, and some basic qualities were imparted thus early for his future work. This is not to say that God cannot do a sovereign work in the most unpromising and unprovidential material, but he is not ordinarily prodigal and wasteful in the use of the miraculous, and generally works from a long-term point of view. In other words, a wise spiritual adviser may well be able to say, knowing a man's history and spiritual experience, "I do not think that this urge within you to become a preacher is from God"; or conversely, even in face of liabilities and disadvantages which, humanly speaking, might seem to be contra-indications, say nevertheless, "In spite of these things, I believe God is truly calling you to his service, and I think you should go forward."

Not that the guidance and advice of the wisest of counsellors is infallible. We are fallible mortals and even a very wise man could be wrong in his judgment, or his judgment, made in all good faith, be overruled by the sovereign will of God. All the same, such counsel should cause a man to give fresh, prayerful consideration to the whole issue.

Secondly, an even more important outward indication — one could go even further and call it a seal — of a man's call to the ministry is that he should already be showing some evidence of aptitude and unction upon him as a future preacher. The Apostle Paul was showing such signs and evidences of fruitfulness long before his commission to service recorded in Acts 13:1-4. If a man is called of God from his mother's womb for service, the "shape of things to come" may well manifest itself in some significant prophetic way even before the call is heard and obeyed (sometimes so clearly that discerning people may begin to surmise that he is earmarked for a holy calling).

The voice of the Church also plays its part in the call to the ministry, and this must be considered in two different ways.

On the one hand, it is the Church's duty and responsibility to test a man's call, to satisfy herself that it is authentic; and when she does, this serves to confirm the call to the man himself. The manner in which the Church does this, and the criteria employed in doing so, may vary in different communions. But it is certain that great and increasing care must be exercised in order to come to a position where it is possible to echo the spirit of the apostolic pronouncement in Acts 15:28: "It has seemed good to the Holy Spirit and to us . . .". Many deliberations may doubtless be involved before that point can be reached, with careful assessment of intellectual, emotional, psychological and spiritual capabilities.

Above all, in such an assessment, the candidate's conviction about his call must be paramount. If he is not sure about that, then, however suitable and promising in all other respects he may be, the Church has not only the right, but also the duty, to call his candidature in question. "If the trumpet give an uncertain sound, who shall prepare himself to the battle?" (1 Cor 14:8 KJV). The Church cannot afford, through lack of continuing vigilance by assessment boards, to run the risk alluded to so forcibly by G. Adam Smith:

> "There are men who pass into the ministry by social pressure or the opinion of the circles they belong to, and there are men who adopt the profession simply because it is on the line of least resistance. From which false beginnings rise the spent

force, the premature stoppages, the stagnancy, the aimlessness and heartlessness, which are the scandals of the professional ministry and the weakness of the Christian Church in our day. Men who drift into the ministry, as it is certain so many do, become mere ecclesiastical flotsam and jetsam, incapable of giving carriage to any soul across the waters of this life, uncertain of their own arrival anywhere, and of all the waste of their generation, the most patent and disgraceful. God will have no driftwood for His sacrifices, no drift-men for His ministers . . .[5]

On the other hand, it may be asked whether the Church has yet another function in relation to the call to the ministry. The New Testament has a disturbing way of breaking through our neat little systems and exploding them in our faces. What, for example, are we to make of the record in Acts 16:3 of the call Timothy received to the ministry? All that is said is "Paul wanted Timothy to accompany him". There is no record of anything Timothy may have thought about the matter. Paul took the initiative, and that is how Timothy became involved in the work of the gospel.

This raises important and far-reaching questions. Paul could not have acted irresponsibly in this matter: he must have been quite sure of the leading of the Spirit so to have done; but the fact remains that he did so, and his action was confirmed by subsequent events, for Timothy turned out to be an able and faithful minister of the Word. But the question is: What part does an individual, or a representative of the Church, or the Church itself, play in the call to the ministry?

Is there not a case for saying that, given a Church where the Spirit of God is regnant, where the ascended Lord is allowed to be Lord, one of the ways in which he will call men to his work will be by using his Church, or even individuals in the Church, to extend the call to men?

Doubtless this is an undemocratic, authoritarian pattern, but the work of the gospel is sometimes described in the New Testament as warfare, and the Church as an army, and there is nothing democratic about the working of an army. Men are sent to where the battle is fiercest: and when a commander-in-chief wants a particularly critical job done, he does not ask for volunteers so much as send in his crack regiment.

This does not — and can never — mean that direction by the Church takes the place of, or can be a substitute for, the direction

of the Spirit of God. It is always God who commissions. But if
what has been said is valid, there is ground for believing that God
can and does direct and commission men for his work through the
Church's directing and commissioning. We can hardly think that
when Paul decided to take Timothy with him on his second
missionary journey he was presuming to do anything on his own
initiative, but rather under the control of the Spirit of God.
Indeed, the words "It seemed good to us and to the Holy Spirit
. . ." could with effect and with truth be applied to Paul's action in
deciding to take Timothy with him on his missionary labours. The
pronouncements made by the apostles in Acts 15 were made on the
basis of the dominical authority delegated to them in the words of
Matt 16:19, 18:18. If it was valid in principle for them to do so, why
should the principle not be recognised as applicable also in the
matter of the calling to the ministry and the direction of
manpower? If a mature and spiritual Christian, or even the
Church, is able to say with some assurance to a man, "I (we) do not
think you are called to the ministry", why not the same assurance
that another man *is* called?

III

We come now to the question of the spiritual nurture of those who
are called to the ministry of the Word.

It might be thought — and indeed it sometimes seems to be
assumed — that when, and because, a man is genuinely called to
the ministry, he no longer needs nurture for his spiritual life, that
he has "arrived", so far as spiritual realities are concerned, and
that what is now required is primarily theological training and
instruction. Such an assumption — if assumption it is — is so
misleading as to be a distortion of the truth, which is that spiritual
nurture is now for him the one supremely important and essential
consideration. This is not to decry theological training or put a low
estimate upon it: no one reared in a Presbyterian and Reformed
tradition could fail to recognize not only the cardinal value of a
thorough theological education but also the necessity of
continuing theological study in the context of an ongoing
ministry. Nothing that can be said about the prior importance of
spiritual nurture must be allowed to challenge the necessity for
such academic discipline. Nor need it: indeed, one suspects that
where theological illiteracy obtains, the cause lies not in an over-

emphasis on spiritual nurture, but in a neglect of it.

But it is necessary to insist that theological training, however essential for the ministry, does not make the student a man of God. So great a scholar and academic as James Denney, speaking of the essential qualification of the Christian minister as being "a heart pledged to his brethren in the love of Christ", acknowledges that a professional education, even in theology, does not of itself produce this, and that the University and the Divinity Schools can confer no competence here. What he speaks of as the need for "a greater expenditure of soul on their work" is something that only spiritual discipline and nurture can impart to men.[6]

The evidence of Scripture itself is quite decisive in this matter. Moses, man of God, received his spiritual nurture, and was shaped and fashioned for his life's work, in the wilderness; Elijah and Elisha had the schools of the prophets; our Lord's training of the Twelve was designed to lead them into the inner secrets of the spiritual life — he called them "that they should be with him" (Mark 3:14), to live in the intimacies of fellowship with him; and Paul had his "silent years", between the Damascus Road experience, and his commissioning at Antioch as apostle to the Gentiles.

It is this distinction that Paul surely had in mind when he wrote to Timothy, "Take heed *to yourself* and to your teaching" (1 Tim 4:16). The context of the apostle's injunction makes it clear that it is godliness and holiness of life that he has in mind. It can hardly be questioned that for Paul this was central and fundamental for a true and faithful ministry. He speaks of having been put to the test and then entrusted with the gospel (1 Thess 2:4 NEB), in a passage which speaks of his gospel coming "not in word only, but also in power" (1 Thess 1:5) because of what manner of men he and his companions had been among the Thessalonians, and because their behaviour was "holy and righteous and blameless" (1 Thess 2:10) among them. The association of ideas is unmistakeable and incontrovertible. The anointing in Paul's ministry was integrally related to the kind of man he was, and had become.

It is hardly possible not to think in this connection of those "silent years" in his experience, during which he was "withdrawn" from the forefront of Christian work and that at a time when so much was critical and strategic — years in which his soul was sifted and disciplined as it was exposed to the majesty of the divine Word.

One thing should be clear from all this: what a man is determines the quality and worth of all that he does; and what he is depends on what he is prepared to be made by the Word, and on whether he is prepared to allow that inner transformation to take place.

It is this that brings upon a man's words what our forefathers used to speak of as that indefinable unction which distinguishes and separates true preaching from all mere human address. It is a divine anointing, that makes the message preached a thing of grace and power, and makes telling impact on the lives of men. The contrast between this apostolic pattern and what so often obtains in our churches today is an eloquent reminder both of the fact that holding an orthodox position — however impeccably evangelical and reformed — does not of itself guarantee the unction of the Spirit, and of the need for those being prepared for the ministry to be given the kind of spiritual nurture that will make such a ministry possible for them.

This is the real challenge of true preparation for the ministry. We are often tempted to take lower ground, for it is a costly way to live, and substitutes for it are common.

It is here that two avenues of help should be available. On the one hand, it is the responsibility of Presbytery to oversee those in training for the ministry, and wise, discerning and spiritual counsel can do much both to energize young men who may from time to time be under considerable pressures from various directions, and to give them a true sense of direction for their future ministry, in the sense of giving them a *raison d'etre* as preachers of the Word, and the consciousness and conviction that preaching is a full-time task, so that they will not spend fruitless years seeking vainly for a "role" in socio-political activism outwith the commission to preach. The Church itself must bear considerable responsibility for the loss of emphasis on both the centrality and the urgency of preaching, and unless there is a rehabilitation of the biblical emphasis on preaching — of the sort that made P.T. Forsyth say "Preaching is the most distinctive institution in Christianity", and "With its preaching, Christianity stands or falls" — the process of decay in the Christian Church is likely to continue. The minister's task is to minister the Word: this is his priority, and it must *be* a priority with him. A Presbytery which recognizes this to be so, and endeavours with a true spiritual concern to encourage and nurture this in the men in its care, will fulfil a pastoral ministry of immense and incalculable value.

On the other hand — a local congregation, if it is a living, worshipping, praying community, can provide a "life-line" that will link a man with the living God, and afford a richness of fellowship and a possibility of spiritual nurture which in terms of strengthening and encouraging faith will prove simply inestimable. The Divinity student's primary need is not to be introduced to as many different forms and variations of worship and service as possible, however interesting and stimulating these may be, but to be anchored in a loving, caring community of the faithful, where he can sit under a living ministry of the Word.

For there his life will be shaped and fashioned for spiritual fruitfulness; there he will learn that "the earthen vessel" must be broken for the light to show forth (2 Cor 4:7ff KJV), that behind every life that tells for God there is a price that has been paid in costly spiritual discipline and consecration, in order to become broken bread and poured out wine for the life of the world. He will learn that the message of Christ crucified can be preached effectively only by crucified men.

NOTES

1. κλητος, "called" (of God), includes, according to Sanday and Headlam, both the idea of a call being given and that of the call being responded to.
2. Von Allmen, *Preaching and Congregation* p.15
3. cf J. Edwin Orr, *The Second Evangelical Awakening* p.59, quoting the United Presbyterian magazine Vol IV, p.333 (1860)
4. This is echoed in other parts of Scripture. Jeremiah speaks (Jer 20:9) of the urge to preach as a fire in his bones compelling him to speak for God.
5. Commentary on Isaiah Vol 1 (Expositor's Bible) p.77
6. Commentary on 2 Corinthians (Expositor's Bible) pp.68, 69

3
Theological training and parish work

JOHN R. GRAY

In every age and in every country where the Christian Faith has been accepted the priest or minister has had functions fairly well defined and generally understood: to proclaim the truth of God as it is given to him, to celebrate the Sacraments, to teach the young, to provide the ordinances of religion (marriage, burial and the like), to comfort the sad, to visit the sick and the dying, to take his part in the affairs of his local congregation or wider denomination. To all of this there has been added in recent years such varied tasks as editing a parish magazine, acting as school or industrial chaplain, appearing on radio or television and entering into ecumenical relations with other Christian denominations. No man is able to perform such a range of tasks really well. Some will excel in one field of activity and some in another, but every minister can be expected to make an honest attempt in each of these areas — to obtain a pass mark, as it were. Most will do something well. An obvious alternative to the all-purpose ministry is to have a team with specialised abilities and training — one to act as pastor, another as preacher, another as Christian educator, and so on. The solution is not practicable in rural areas or where Christians are few. At any rate, it is the man who has become known and trusted as pastor who will be listened to as preacher. The man who celebrates the Sacraments will bring an extra grace when he visits the sick or comforts the mourner.

In Scotland — and this book is written mainly from a Scottish perspective — the work of the ministry is at once restricted and deepened by the parish system which prevails here, as in England and many countries of Europe. By this system, the whole country is divided into areas, in each of which there is one minister, with or without assistance, whose primary duty it is to care for all the people who live within its bounds so far as they are willing to accept his ministry. It is sometimes said that the parish system has broken down due to the movements of population. It is true that it is not possible in large cities to allocate a community to every minister, nor in the country a minister to every community, but as a method of evangelism the parish system has no equal. The minister who will systematically visit every home in his parish, so far as time and strength allow, will have a richly rewarding ministry, whether in the centre of the city, a town or a rural area. Of course, there are other specialised types of ministry besides that of the parish minister — chaplains to the forces, overseas missionaries, and the like — but the basic unit of the Church in Scotland is the parish and most of those in the ministry will be parish ministers.

I

What tasks fill the parish minister's week and life and what kind of theological education will fit him for those tasks? These are questions which need constant re-examination, for while the basic tasks are as have been outlined above, considerable adjustment will be called for to meet the changing circumstances of every successive age and for every different parish. In the parish which the writer knows best there is an average of at least one funeral a week, a marriage and a baptism every two weeks. The minister pays at least thirty pastoral calls a week, edits a parish magazine once a month, and acts as chaplain to two schools. Edinburgh committees, the Presbytery, teaching a probationer assistant, occasional appearances on radio and television, Kirk Session meetings, First Communicant classes, speaking in other congregations, spasmodic journalistic efforts and reading take up the rest of his time. Ministers in other sorts of parishes will be forced to have different priorities as they face different problems. A denominationally homogeneous Highland parish is a very different thing from a congregation in a University city where young people are continually confronted with the claims of humanism, agnosticism or even the doctrines of Mr. Moon. In the latter situation, the minister will need to be able not only to declare the Faith that is in him but to defend it over against those who deny it or interpret it differently. Since however the movement of population is now so great and since young people nearly all must seek higher education or training in the cities and since at any rate television and radio have invaded almost every home in the country, the contrast between the varying types of parish grows ever less.

In any First Communicants class, the question of other Faiths and the relationship of the Christian Faith to them will almost inevitably arise. Mixed marriages are more frequent than ever before and demand an increasing awareness of the similarities and differences between Protestantism and Romanism as well as those between Christianity and other Religions. The meaning of the Sacraments and Ordinances of the Church now have to be explained more fully than ever before. The days when you "had to" be baptised and "had to" go to Church on Sunday and in due course "had to join the Church" and be married there are gone. There is a demand for the need and purposes of each of these activities to be explained and for their relevance to be proved. There are a bewildering series of ethical dilemmas to be faced: to marry or not to marry divorced people — and if not, to show why not from first principles — what attitude to take to such issues as abortion, or the artificial prolongation of life of the terminally ill. What of the admission of refugees to Britain? There will be few pastoral visits where one or other of these ethical questions do not crop up. Those who ask them will listen very closely to the sort of answer given. They may not accept what the minister says unthinkingly but they will expect what he says to be based on some recognisable theological principle. Always the age old questions will be propounded to him: "What comes after death?" "Should children be left to make up their own minds about religion?" "Why is there evil?" "In what sense is Jesus the Son of God?" "Is prayer answered?" Hardly a day will pass without these matters being raised and those who raise them will demand answers not based on the latest TV chat programme nor on the minister's own limited experience but on the revelation of God's purposes in Jesus Christ.

Questions will arise in the homes of the bereaved, the sick and the perplexed, in class room and in Bible class which will drive the minister back to the coherent and intelligible interpretation of the

Faith he once was taught if that has been his rare good fortune, to books which he has been taught to use and above all to his knees where he has been taught to pray. He will be of no use to his people if all he can give is a summary of the views of several theologians ancient and modern, or a balance of probabilities. His people will expect him to have worked out his own basic beliefs and their consequences and to be able to state them positively and intelligibly. They also have the right to expect that these beliefs will be in general accord with those of the denomination he has chosen to serve.

This does not mean of course that the minister is to have a closed mind. Having worked out for himself a basic theology and having sought ordination in a church with the general position of which he finds himself in broad agreement, he will yet keep himself abreast, so far as he can, with modern scholarship and theological trends. He will get most out of the time he can spend in study, however, if by the time he leaves University he has arrived at a clearly defined although not, of course, rigid position. Indeed it is essential for him to do so for, from the beginning of his ministry, he will be confronted with both pastoral decisions and with theological problems on which he will be expected to give clear and helpful guidance.

In view of these facts, it would appear to be best if systematic instruction on the basis of one coherent theological system were given at the undergraduate stage rather than a pot-pourri of many. The stimulus provided by studying other systems, the dialogue with other Faiths, will be most helpful against the background of one agreed system. Those who emerge from theological training thoroughly confused will not only find themselves inadequate for the job for which after all they are being paid, but will only become more confused by subsequent reading and study for which only minimal amounts of time will be available. Those who wish to go the second theological mile must begin by walking every step of the first.

II

In the light of its knowledge of what young ministers will be asked to do, it is the obvious duty of the Church to ensure that there is an adequate supply of candidates for the holy ministry, that the selection of those applying is made in the light of the work they will have to do and that those selected are properly trained for the varied tasks they will so soon face.

This training can be done in one of three ways — entirely by the Universities, or partly by the Universities and partly by Church Training Colleges, or entirely by Church Training Colleges or Seminaries. Of necessity, the third was the method adopted by the United Presbyterian and Free Churches of Scotland before their Union in 1900 and by the United Free Church prior to the Union of 1929. Colleges were maintained by the Church, professors were appointed by the Church and courses were prescribed by the Church, although individual students might concurrently study for and obtain the B.D. degree offered by the Universities. The system had much to commend it. Those chosen to be professors were those who had a good knowledge of the ministry and who had given proof of their devotion to the Gospel and of their love of the Church. For the most part, they remained closely integrated with the life of the Church and were indeed looked to for leadership in its courts. They were constantly made aware of its changing needs. The fact that they came relatively late to teaching theology and continued to take their full share of preaching and of the work of Presbytery and Assembly does not seem to have limited their scholarly output, as names like T.M. Lindsay, George Adam Smith, J.F. McFadyen, James Moffat and James Denney would seem to prove. Indeed, considering that for the most part these professors were without assistance, it is amazing that they published more works of notable scholarship than most of their modern counterparts.

The second system of training for the ministry was that of the old Church of Scotland, where the students were taught by professors of the University, whose Chairs were mostly of great antiquity. The teaching of those professors was supplemented to a limited extent by Pastoral Institutes of various kinds and by an apprenticeship system with tuition by senior ministers. The great advantage of this system was that the Faculty of Divinity was closely integrated with other Faculties and that there was an interchange of ideas with students of other disciplines.

At the Union of the Church of Scotland and the United Free Church in 1929, the Chairs in the former United Free Colleges were added to those in the University, with the exception initially of the Chairs of Practical Theology in Glasgow and Aberdeen, about which various special arrangements were made, the theory apparently being that these Chairs were too practical and career-oriented to be included in a University — a queer suggestion when one thinks of Chairs of subjects such as Surgery, Naval Architecture and Forestry. Appointments to all Chairs in the Faculties of Divinity were to be made by a Board of Nomination, drawn equally from the Church and the University concerned. The University retained the right to appoint after a year in the event of disagreement. In 1952 the two Church Chairs were brought into line with the other Chairs of Theology, as regards the method of appointment, except that the right to appoint after a year was not in their case reserved by the Universities.

The entire revenues of all Church Chairs except those in Pastoral Theology were made over the Universities. Subsequently the buildings of Trinity College, Glasgow and New College, Edinburgh were handed over also, although some right of redemption was retained for New College. The Principalships of the Colleges in Glasgow, Edinburgh and Aberdeen were retained, the idea being that the professors appointed as Principals would represent the Church to the University concerned and would also exercise some pastoral concern over the spiritual life of the students. All of this worked fairly well at first, but in recent years there have been certain significant changes. In the first place, an increasing number of clergymen not of the Church of Scotland — Anglicans, Methodists, Greek Orthodox and Roman Catholics — have been appointed to Chairs and Lectureships, the most recent appointment being that of an Irish-American married Roman Catholic priest or ex-priest to the Thomas Chalmers Chair of Theology in Edinburgh University.

A second tendency has been to appoint men, even to Chairs of Practical Theology, with little or no experience of the parish ministry. It is not that parish ministers are discriminated against; simply that the main criterion for appointments is the amount of work published and research done, not the ability to train future ministers, nor a knowledge of the work for which they are being trained.

A third tendency has been to treat Theology in a more and more narrowly intellectual way, almost divorced from faith or from the life of the Church. God has sometimes been treated as an idea to be considered or a word to by analysed, rather than as the Lord who may properly be approached only on one's knees, in prayer, in worship and obedience. The impossibility of looking upon God in

the same way as a biologist looks on the frog he is dissecting has not
always been realised. Those who teach Church History, Old or
New Testament, may claim something of the same kind of
objectivity for their disciplines as teachers of Botany or Geology.
The Bible can be studied in much the same way as secular History.
Yet it is inconceivable that several University teachers would be
paid to study and to teach one book, but for that Book's vital
importance to the Christian Religion; and Church History could
well be taught as a department of ordinary History, but for its
relevance to the Church of today and tomorrow.

A fourth cause of concern is that some men are being appointed
to teach theological subjects, or are being continued as teachers
who profess no belief in God, who rarely if ever attend public
worship, and who show an indifference to Christian moral
standards in their lives.

III

How is the Church to face this situation? In the first place, it
should seek a remedy within the present arrangement. It can fairly
point out that the majority of the people in Scotland are associated
in some way with the Church of Scotland, which has over two
million baptised persons. A great many of the unbaptised would also
claim, if pressed, to belong to it. This can be checked by taking the
statistics of those entering hospitals or the armed forces, or by the
numerous surveys which have been made. In view of this
predominance and since the Universities are maintained at the
public expense, there would seem to be a very good case for
expecting the Faculties of Theology to provide the sort of training
which the Church judges to be necessary and desirable for its
ministers. Certainly, if the Faculties of Theology were to train
men unable to perform the work of the ministry or if there were no
churches for the men they train to serve in, the Faculties
themselves would very soon and very properly be abolished. Those
who provide what nobody wants or who fail to provide what is
wanted will sooner or later in the academic as in the business
world find themselves without a job.

The only justification for the existence and maintenance of
Faculties of Theology is the existence of the Church. Teachers of
Theology should therefore be extremely sensitive to the changing
needs of the Church and responsive to them. Since the Roman

Catholic Church, the only other Church of a significant size in Scotland, makes its own provision for the training of the priesthood, the Church in this context can be assumed to be the Church of Scotland. The *raison d'etre*, therefore, of the Faculties of Divinity in the Scottish Universities is in fact to be found largely in the Church of Scotland. It is the Church which provides the students and provides work for the students once they are trained. If the Church were to disappear, it would not be long before the Faculties of Divinity followed suit.

If the Universities — or any one of them — refuse to heed the requests of the Church, the Church must take whatever steps to remedy the situation it deems to be necessary. It could withdraw its students from one or more of the Universities where training was found to be unsatisfactory. It could set up its own Training College for the ministry in one of the Universities, making use of such University classes as were taught by teachers of whom it could approve. It could enter into arrangements with the Colleges of independent Presbyterian Churches in Ireland or Wales or with Westminster College, Cambridge. It could require from its students a supplementary year at a Church College. It is, of course, to be hoped that none of these measures will be necessary. There are some splendid churchmen among the teachers of Theology in Scotland, as in every country, and they are eager to ensure that, as in the past, the Universities meet the needs of the Church.

Perhaps the time has come for some thorough re-examination of the relationship between the Church and the Faculties of Theology in the Universities and perhaps also for the Church to ask itself if it is prepared to undertake once again complete responsibility for the training of its own ministers with all that that involves in the way of cost, loss of academic status and of the stimulus of other University Faculties.

An interesting suggestion was recently made by a retired Professor of Medicine that all Chairs of Theology should be Clinical Chairs, as it were. He pointed out that on the day he ceased to be in charge of a hospital ward he had to resign his Chair. It would have been impossible for him to teach Medicine without continuing to practise it. The fact that Professors of Medicine, Obstetrics, Medical Jurisprudence and other subjects must spend much time in clinical work does not seem to prevent them from giving excellent instruction in lectures, guiding research work of importance and publishing both in learned society journals and in larger works. Theological education might possibly be better, and it would certainly gain in relevance, if those appointed to academic posts were required to continue as parish ministers, adequate assistance being provided for them in their parishes. Certainly, it is essential that the training for the ministry be directed towards the work which the minister will be required to do. Perhaps the truth about the Resurrection can only become clear as one sits with a husband at the side of his dying wife. Infant Baptism is better considered by one who is baptising babies as part of his duty than by one who must view the matter *in vacuo*. Perhaps it is time for Practical Theology to be regarded not as the Cinderella but as the Queen of the various theological disciplines towards the requirements of which they should all be directed. Christ did not call academics to teach but fishers to become fishers of men. Christianity is not theoretical but essentially and inescapably applied, and the studies of those who are to be ministers should be directed towards that application.

If the ministry is to be adequate for the challenge of the 1980s and beyond much more thought must be given to how ministers are to be trained. If disagreements on policy should lead to a more satisfactory state of affairs, they will not have been in vain.

No better conclusion of this chapter could be devised than to quote some sentences culled from a book by Professor Norman W. Porteous, former Principal of New College, Edinburgh. In a splendid chapter, "Theology in Church and University", he says among other wise things, "The theological affirmations and denials of the Church have to be lived as well as spoken . . . We must think, so to say, not only with our intellects but with our actions." "Theology is always in danger of becoming irrelevant . . . That is why dogmatics has to be Church dogmatics." "The very language of theology only comes alive when we are face to face with human need." "The presupposition controlling our ultimate theological task is that God has revealed himself in human history, a presupposition which we can only make on the basis of faith." "Anyone without commitment on his part may interest himself in theological writings. It is impossible for anyone to think theologically outside the relationship in which he acknowledges the claim of the living God upon his mind and will."[1] These are wise words which, if acted upon, could lead to fruitful co-operation rather than sterile strife between the Church and the Faculties of Theology.

NOTE

1. N.W. Porteous, *Living the Mystery* pp.171-176

4

Training the whole Church for Ministry

DAVID F. WRIGHT

I

The 1979 General Assembly of the Church of Scotland approved a motion

> "noting with concern that a number of professors and lecturers in our Scottish Divinity Faculties, who are responsible for preparing students for the ministry, have no personal experience of the parish ministry, of chaplaincy work or mission".

More than one of the apparently factual elements in this deliverance are open to question, but more seriously it suffers from a basic ambiguity. Who may be regarded as having "personal experience of the parish ministry, of chaplaincy work or mission"? If we may leave aside the admittedly more specialised field of "chaplaincy work", we must ask whether "personal experience of the parish ministry" is predicable only of ordained "ministers" in parochial charges, that is, of those whom other traditions and sometimes our own call "parish clergy". Is "personal experience of mission" similarly a qualification enjoyed only by people who have engaged in mission overseas, and then only in an ordained capacity?

Since the ramifications involved in pursuing the question of "mission" are complex and far-reaching, we will concentrate on "the parish ministry". Most commissioners at the Assembly will probably have understood this phrase as synonymous with "the ministry" mentioned earlier in the motion. Let us restate our central question: Are the only people (or Christians or members of the Church) who may be spoken of as having "personal experience of the parish ministry" ordained "ministers" who are or have been in congregational charges, i.e., parochial clergy? What of the elders, the Bible class leaders, the Sunday school superintendents and teachers, the Woman's Guild office-bearers — does their service not count as "personal experience of the parish ministry"?

Of course in one sense anyone who has had any dealings with the local kirk at all may be said to have had "personal experience of the parish ministry", whether the nominal Church member wanting a baby baptized or the most faithful regular who is always in his or her place on a Sunday morning. Theirs will be the experience of recipients or consumers or clients of "the parish ministry". Yet no one will suppose that this is the kind of "personal experience" the Assembly noted the lack of with concern. Nevertheless even this almost flippant understanding of the phrase under examination provokes us to ask with all seriousness some searching questions of traditional "training for the ministry". Why has it been so little informed by consumer research? Why, for example, have homiletics (the science of preaching) remained for the most part innocent of investigations into the effects of preaching — how, and how much, hearers in the pew actually learn or "take away" from sermons, perhaps by comparison with other methods of teaching? What are "students for the ministry" taught about the observed and measured impact of different approaches to the tricky problems of baptismal discipline, especially the impact on the parents involved? How far is training consciously influenced by successful ministries, i.e. patterns of ministry which have proved successful by publicly recognisable (if not unanimously acknowledged) criteria in particular situations?

In what is sometimes called "ministerial formation" the interplay between academic study and practical experience is increasingly given high evaluation. I need only refer to the structure of Edinburgh University's new Diploma in Ministry which comprises one year spent largely in fieldwork placements in parishes, hospitals, etc., followed by a second year devoted chiefly to biblical and theological study enriched by the previous year's experience. But notice that in such a pattern, as in refresher courses or post-experience training, the experience that sensitizes theological reflection is mostly that of the trainees themselves, i.e., parochial clergy or clergy-to-be. Rarely is what we may call the consumers' experience of the clergy's ministry fed into such training, no doubt partly or largely because it has not often been made the object of rigorous research. As a result we have the strange situation that preaching is taught by those who rarely listen to sermons, and how to visit the sick by healthy visitors rather than sick patients. There is clearly much territory here for the religious psychologist, sociologist and educationalist to possess, territory which should yield valuable raw material for training ordinands and ordained. In the process their training will become to a greater degree a training that takes place within the Church and at the hands of the Church.

Some readers will doubtless object to my use of the term "consumers" — as though the relationship between "minister" and people were reducible to that of producer and consumer! Unfortunately the average congregation in the main functions merely as a body of consumers of parish ministry (and in one significant respect almost entirely so, as we shall see). There is no denying that we are dealing with an area in which language is a sensitive issue. Other readers may have felt uneasy at my reference to "ministers" as "clergy" and at the implication it carries that the Church consists of clergy on the one hand and laity on the other. Objection is rightly made in the Kirk from time to time that such a distinction is foreign to the Reformed tradition. The whole Church, it is insisted, is the *laos,* the "people" of God. We must therefore resist the theological implications of the language of "clergy" and "laity". Nevertheless this language has its value, not least in the Church of Scotland. It makes explicit and inescapable what more conventional usage in the Kirk often disguises (and is the more harmful for so disguising), namely, *the Kirk's seeming inability to break free of restrictive notions of "ministry",* notions which are often clericalist and at times even priestly or sacerdotal in flavour.

It is here that we touch on the most worrying aspect of the ambiguous Assembly deliverance with which we started. It assumes Theological Faculties to be places where students are prepared for "the ministry", which appears to mean "the parish ministry" (or even more specialized field of "chaplaincy work or mission"). The desire is apparently implied for training for "the parish ministry" to constitute the *raison d'etre* of the faculties, and for this training to be in the hands of people experienced as parish "ministers". A restrictive notion of "ministry" is thereby fastened on the parish Church and then applied to transform the Faculties of Divinity into Seminaries — which they have never been in Scotland.

It could perhaps be argued in defence of the Assembly's statement that "the ministry" is merely convenient shorthand and should not be read as implying a denial of the ministry of the whole people of God. But such a defence is unconvincing, for the recognition that "parish ministry" is and must be fulfilled by numerous Church members besides ordained men and women must give rise to another, that the training of the ministry cannot logically — theo-logically — be restricted only to the ordained.

What is at stake here is the seriousness with which we take the New Testament, rather than ecclesiastical tradition, in constructing our doctrine of ministry. The ground has been gone over often enough in recent years, yet New Testament perspectives seem sadly lacking among us. Jesus Christ is the only true minister of the grace of God to men. In so far as his ministry is committed to and exercized in the Church, it belongs to the Church as a whole, the Church as his Body. This ministry is accomplished through a rich variety of ministries which are essentially the gifts (charismata) of Christ to his Body, not the peculiar possession of individuals (1 Cor 12:4-6). Such a diversity of ministries is indeed constitutive of the Church as Christ's Body. The New Testament congregations knew of no single human functionary or officer called "the minister". Indeed, it is a strange irony that among the varied range of ministerial functions or gifts attested in the earliest Churches, "the minister" and "the ministry" are conspicuously absent (except as possible translations for "deacon" and "the diaconate") — for *all* were ministers of Christ and his gospel: evangelists, teachers, pastors or shepherds, presbyters or elders, heralds or preachers, bishops or overseers or superintendents, deacons, governors or rulers, healers, prophets, administrators (organizers?), and others still. Not all of these designations are necessarily exclusive of all others; fluidity of practice and title was the order of the day. Nor can it be assumed without question that all of the charismata or ministries listed, let alone others which sound unfamiliar to most of us (the working of miracles, the declaration of wisdom and of knowledge, speaking in tongues . . .), are intended for every congregation of Christ's people for all time. But the fundamental thrust remains unaffected: the Body of Christ is built up by the harmonious functioning of all its parts (Eph 4:16), through the Spirit's distribution of gifts to each member for the common good (1 Cor 12:7).

II

It is against this New Testament back cloth that the Kirk's use and wont must be critically surveyed. The habit of speaking of "minister" and "ministry" exclusively of the single person uniquely charged with responsibility for dispensing the Word and Sacraments in the congregation must be accounted singularly unfortunate and damagingly restrictive. It is unfortunate for the obvious reason that this particular usage is not to be found among the several possible designations evidenced in the New Testament. It also carries the unhappy implication that one person, "the minister", combines in himself the whole spectrum of necessary biblical ministries, that he or she is called to be teacher, evangelist, pastor, baptizer and much else rolled into one and *must be trained accordingly*. We seem to have forgotten that Calvin, following the Strasbourg Reformers, distinguished at least four orders of ministry — pastor, teacher, deacon, elder.

The Church's traditional use of "minister" and "ministry" has also proved restrictive, perhaps the major contributory factor in the Church's backwardness in developing not only the ministry of the laity and patterns of ecumenical ministry but also supplementary forms of clerical ministry. Why has the Church of Scotland so little progress to show in the areas of auxiliary ministry, non-stipendiary or part-time ministry, group ministry or team ministry? Why has the considerable element of diversity of ministries built into the Church's Presbyterian polity in the form of elders and managers or deacons so rarely realized more than a fraction of its potential? There is in the average congregation a great gulf fixed between "the minister" and the rest, whether elders or "ordinary" members. Only a very exceptional elder will think of his responsibility as a Christian ministry. If one person is "the minister", it is not surprising if ministry is seen as his job and his alone. After all he is the professional, the finished product of a lengthy and expensive training, full-time, earning his living as a stipendiary "minister". No wonder the shouldering of congregational responsibility for ministry is so difficult to promote! And often when it does develop, those involved regard themselves as helping "the minister" in *his* work rather than fulfilling by the gift of the risen Christ ministries of his Body in their own right.

Further aspects of our ministerial malaise need to be diagnosed for its full gravity to be realized. In the Church of Scotland, a congregation "calls" a man or woman to be its "minister". The person so called will in most cases have been previously unknown to almost everyone in the congregation. Not only will the congregation normally have done nothing to produce their new "minister" (except very indirectly by means of contributions to central funds of the Church), it will probably have done nothing in living memory to produce any candidates for any congregation's "ministry". That is to say, most congregations are consumers of "ministers", not producers. When needed, "ministers" are available from the Church at large, lists of eligible candidates are circulated, others apply or are personally recommended. The congregation does not have to do anything other than choose and pay. (Procedures for filling vacancies have reminded many observers of the style of the consumer in the shopping centre).

What this system so readily discourages is the sense of congregational responsibility for the task of ministry. A vacancy is invariably an inactive period. A "minister"-less congregation is barely a congregation at all (see further below), a headless torso passing its life in a kind of limbo and given a periodic kiss-of-life by an interim moderator or more sustained respiration by a locum tenens. And if for one reason or another the wider Church decrees that it cannot be allowed a "minister", its very existence as a congregation will be in jeopardy. "The Presbytery confirm the view of its Readjustments Committee that a minister cannot be spared to enable . . . to continue as an independent congregation".[1] The Church is thus made so dependent on "the ministry" that without it a congregation must cease to exist. When the sole legitimate Church-sustaining form of ministry is the full-time, ordained, stipendiary "minister", the relation between Church and ministry has fallen into of something not far short of heresy.

How differently primitive Christianity developed! As a result of mission preaching, congregations were gathered in which ministries of various kinds were exercised, by the gift of the Spirit of the exalted Christ, as Paul understood it, and in due course persons of proven worth *from among their own ranks* were recognized or designated as presbyters or deacons or bishops or prophets or teachers ... ministry was a function of the congregation, ministries were nurtured within the congregation. The Churches were in this sense self-sustaining, self-supporting. (It is salutary to note that in contemporary Kirk usage "self-supporting" has a largely financial connotation.) The contrast with the modern Church could scarcely be more marked.

Now I do not want to suggest that the importing of "ministers" from outside the congregation has nothing to commend it. If I may single out merely one benefit, it is an arrangement which in my view maintains the catholicity of the Church. But I am not here concerned to argue the pro's and con's of different patterns of ecclesiastical organization. I am intent rather on highlighting the crippling handicap that we in the Kirk have to overcome if the Church's whole ministerial resources are to be mobilized for its contemporary mission.

One further aspect of the restrictive notion of "ministry" that plagues the Church is the astonishing fact that in the average congregation "the minister" is the only person (apart perhaps from the organist) who has received any formal training for his task. The gulf between "minister" and the rest is at its widest on the education front. In most congregations elders are untrained, Sunday school teachers are untrained, indeed nobody is trained for anything. The systematic attempts that are now being made to promote Christian education in the congregation have to compete with the illiteracy of past neglect. By contrast "ministers" receive up to seven years' full-time education largely off the job in a university. During some of their student years and in their months as licensed probationers, candidates are involved in the work of congregations, but it remains true that most congregations in the Church have no experience of students-in-training. The whole process takes place beyond their ken. To judge by the repeated comments of New College students, even Presbyteries are often only minimally involved. Thus not only are "ministers" normally the only trained congregational personnel, but also their lengthy training takes place in a world widely removed from congregational experience.

III

How then should the Church's ministry be re-formed? It may be utopian to expect a revision of terminology, but the liberating effect of the right kind of change would in my judgment prove so considerable in the long term that the attempt must be made. The Church should cease to talk without qualification of "the ministry" and "the minister" when what it means is the regularly trained, ordained presbyter, normally full-time and stipendiary. What term should replace "the minister"? An obvious candidate is "the presbyter", even though it is the same word, transliterated but not translated, as "elder". The use of the same word in two forms might be acceptable as indicating the distinction yet parity between the teaching elder and the ruling elder. Some, however, are likely to see the different form "presbyter" as obscuring or even denying the Presbyterian fundamental that the presbyterate is but one order, incorporating both "ministers" and elders.

No functional term like "pastor" or "preacher" or "teacher" stands much chance of acceptance, if only for the poor reason that for most people "the ministry" incorporates all these functions and others besides. More gingerly, lacking the courage of my conviction, I suggest that primitive Christianity offers one obvious answer — the term "bishop" or one of its equivalents as translations of the Greek *episkopos*, "overseer" and "superintendent". The primitive Christian bishop was indeed the chief presbyter of a group or team of presbyters leading the ministry of normally a single congregation. "Bishop" seems tailor-made to replace "minister". Yet one fears that the entail of ancient controversy and modern ecumania will not allow such a suggestion much of an innings. We may have to opt for some more colourless title like "president" or "leader", which can both cite some New Testament support.

In any case no such change will be of any avail unless it is followed by a congregational assumption of the ministry of the Church. *The honoured designations "minister" and "ministry" must die as the prerogative of an individual in order to take on new life as the commission of the congregation.* The transference must also be accompanied by renewed study of the doctrine and practice of ministry in the New Testament. In this exercise we should not disdain the insights rediscovered by the charismatic movement.[2]

The comprehensive aim of ministerial reformation must be nothing less than an all-member ministry. As a major contribution to this end the educational apartheid in the Church must be abolished. The division that separates training for "the ministry" from other training for ministry in the Church, even from training for other kinds of specialized ministry, should be transcended. It is difficult to justify on practical grounds, and impossible on theological, the quite separate arrangements that operate in the Kirk for training deaconesses and the new male diaconate on the one hand and "ministers" on the other. Progress here will require the resources of the Divinity Faculties to be as flexible as possible to service the training of specialized ministries, whether the diaconate, personnel destined for overseas mission or "ministers". In turn the training of "ministers" could profitably make use of the staff and facilities of Centres like St. Colm's College, St. Ninian's Training Centre at Crieff, Carberry Tower and the Netherbow in Edinburgh, particularly for specialized short-term workshops in students' vacations or the probationary period.

Furthermore, the Divinity Faculties should be encouraged to intensify their attempts to cater for the educational needs of other expressions of ministry in the Church, especially readers, elders, and Sunday school and Bible class teachers. Theology in the University should be seen to be at the service of the whole membership of the Church, not squeezed into a seminary mould as I fear the Assembly's deliverance considered earlier appeared to want. The Church of Scotland is suffering from an alarming dearth of educated Christian laymen and laywomen, people distinguished in their daily occupations but also skilled at articulating a practical Christian faith within the secular world. (A simple test will prove the point. Try to think of lay members of the Church who might challenge consideration as future Moderators of the General Assembly. I suspect that all the candidates can be counted on the fingers of one hand.) Numerous Church members have attained high qualification and expertise in their own avocations but their Christian understanding remains stunted. For their growth in knowledge of the faith every effort must be made to develop traditional methods — evening classes in particular — and to initiate new ones, such as correspondence courses, week-end seminars and even part-time degrees. Edinburgh University's new Extra-Mural Certificate in Christian Studies may be mentioned as one example among others. Above all the Church should be inviting the Theological Faculties to commit themselves to the task of "theological education by extension".

But if the Divinity Faculties, where traditionally only "ministers" have been trained (this not altogether accurate assumption in the General Assembly's deliverance probably reflects majority opinion in the Church), must be opened up to cater for wider training of Church members and leaders, in turn the training of "ministers" must to a greater extent take place on the job, in the field. If the regular pattern of training for the "ministry" continues to occupy six or seven years, is the time really best spent wholly in university study? I suspect that considerations that are only marginally educational keep the Church bound to the traditional scheme. The new Edinburgh Diploma in Ministry is surely a sign of things to come, with its interweaving of praxis and theological study. It will certainly presage future developments if the Church of Scotland, like other declining Churches in the worn-out Christian West, is humble enough to learn from the vibrant younger Churches of Africa, Asia and Latin America.

It would be highly beneficial, in my view, if all ministerial students *before* studying theology could spend a year or so working in a Scottish parish on a kind of domestic version of the V.S.O. scheme. Too many ordinands embark on theology with appallingly little experience of congregational ministry; some indeed seem to have received a call to "the ministry" without ever having "had a go" at anything that might merit the description of Christian ministry. An added advantage of such a pre-theological year would hopefully be found in involving a greater number of congregations, if only marginally, in the training of "ministers". Indeed on a broader front I foresee considerable profit accruing to the Church, not least in helping to foster a sense of congregational responsibility for ministry, if more of the training of specialized ministers can be earthed in congregational life.

There are clearly different ways of responding to the unease about the training of "ministers" which has been voiced in recent General Assemblies. Some, in my view mistakenly, wish to clamp a tighter discipline on the Faculties of Divinity, in curriculum, teaching staff, worship and personal devotion, community life and so on. A more appropriate and hopeful response would be for the Church itself to ensure a greater church-based content in the course of training. By this I mean not a supplementary course in a

Church seminary, but a lengthier training exposure to the demands of different parochial and congregational situations. It would, I suggest, advance the Church's awareness of and commitment to its whole ministry if more of the training of its specialist ministers took place in those contexts in the life of the Church where their subsequent service will be set. Therefore if on the one hand I envisage a greater involvement of the Theological Faculties in equipping the wider Church for its varied ministries, on the other hand I would welcome as a healthy development a stronger anchorage of training for ordained ministry in the Church at grass-roots level.

For the most part training of the membership of the Church for ministry (cf Eph 4:11-13) must happen in the local congregation. There will always be a need for special courses of training for elders or Sunday school teachers or parish visitors or youth fellowship leaders, but beyond these Christian education has to be vindicated as an activity of the whole congregation, not reserved for the committed core in specially arranged groups. This calls for the main Sunday meeting of the congregation to be given a purposeful educational thrust. The teaching power of the sermon is surely due for rediscovery, especially if it serves to stimulate its hearers to further study and thought. The preacher's use of Scripture in the pulpit should seek to teach his congregation how they may handle Scripture for themselves. Effective teaching sermons will therefore encourage a measure of independence in those who listen attentively, so that they begin to learn on their own.

Beyond the sermon the range of further possibilities is considerable — from the all-age Christian education so well developed in the U.S.A. and by some Baptist Churches in Scotland, to the use of teaching aids like overhead projectors, the circulation of duplicated summaries or questions for self-programmed learning, the substitution of two or three briefer instructions for the normal sermon, and the incorporation where appropriate of the contribution of other members of the congregation. If Christ's Church makes bodily growth only through the harmonious interdependence of the various ministries with which it is equipped, why is there so little scope for the schoolteacher, the widow, the nurse, the social worker, the young mother, the student and many another to speak their word of wisdom and knowledge before the congregation?

One thing is certain: the ways and means will not be found lacking once the vision is present. The resources available to the Church for congregational education are increasing all the time — personnel, programmes, materials, a burgeoning Christian booktrade, plus the help offered by bodies like the National Sunday School Union, the Scripture Union, the National Bible Society, by institutions such as the Colleges of Education, the Faculties of Theology, the Church's own Centres already mentioned and interdenominational ones like the Bible Training Institute in Glasgow. But what is needed is the vision of a whole Church, a whole congregation trained and committed to its corporate ministry of witness and care in the community. The burden of this chapter is that such a vision requires a thorough recasting of the Church's approach to ministry.

The prospect of such a re-formation of ministry may be felt as a threat by some ordained ministers. To others it will surely be welcome as heralding their liberation from tasks for which they are not fitted, in order to devote themselves to those aspects of ministry for which they are genuinely gifted. No longer should it be incumbent on every "minister" to be good at everything. Rather it will become his or her distinctive role to enable others to develop their own ministries within the congregation, like the player-manager of a football team. Equipping the Church for ministry should be enough of a challenge for most candidates for such a post.

NOTES

1. Edinburgh Presbytery *Minutes*, 1979
2. cf David Watson, *I Believe in the Church* 1978

5

Catholic faith, ecumenism and theological education

GEORGE YULE

The centre of the Christian faith is the Incarnation. From this man's salvation comes and with it our knowledge of God as Father, Son and Holy Spirit. This is the heart of the Church's proclamation and hence it must be what Theological Faculties explore and elucidate, so that ministers may be better equipped to understand and proclaim the truth of the Catholic Faith.

I

The Reformation basically was a rediscovery of certain facets of christology which had become obscured in the legalism and pelagianism of much Mediaeval theology and practice. Luther's rediscovery of *sola gratia* was an essential aspect of the Catholic understanding of the incarnation. A failure to keep central what Luther emphasised has led to new forms of legalism, moralism and pelagianism which differ only in outward form from many of their Mediaeval predecessors.

For so many, the Reformation is seen primarily in terms of the reform of abuses. But not for Luther. Writing to Erasmus in the controversy over free will he said, "Moreover I praise you highly for this also, that unlike all the rest you alone have attacked the real issues, and have not wearied me with irrelevancies about the papacy, purgatory, indulgences and such trifles".[1] Let others spend their time over reforms, Luther would concentrate on "the knotty problems" — "How do you love God with your heart and soul and mind and strength and your neighbour as yourself?" "One thing only is necessary for the Christian life, righteousness and freedom," he wrote. "That one thing is the most holy Word of God the Gospel of Christ . . . You may ask then what is the Word of God, and how shall it be used since there are so many words of God? . . . The Word is the Gospel concerning his Son, who was made flesh, suffered, rose from the dead and was glorified through the Spirit who sanctifies".[2] This was one way in which he expressed the fact that the work of our salvation is due to the sovereign grace of God alone, but he did this so richly and so variously that illumination was cast on many facets of the Christian life; but however expressed, it always revolved around the grace of God given to us in Jesus Christ. Unlike some later Lutheran and Reformed theologians, forgiveness for Luther never stood alone as it were as some forensic transaction. It is for him always connected with "life and salvation". This happens because Christ comes to us, deals with us and enters into fellowship with us. "He comes," says Luther "not poor and destitute — he brings with him everything that he is, has and can do." He gives himself to us "that we may possess him so completely, that all he has and owns becomes ours". The life of faith is a life in Christ in the Spirit.[3]

This central insight of Luther is an essential part of the Catholic faith. If God is the loving Holy Trinity, and if man is as self-centred as St. Augustine showed, so that it was necessary for the Son of God truly to become our fellow man for our salvation as the ancient creeds declare, then the only way to express this is *sola gratia*. For this spells out the cost of our redemption and sums up the best theological reflection upon the Incarnation of the previous centuries.

He explored deeply the anti-pelagian stance of St. Augustine and showed that good works can only come from a heart overflowing with gratitude (the reflex of *sola gratia*). Whereas Augustine had seen that idolatory could consist in being curved over the good things of this world and not just the bad things, Luther showed that one could make one's religious strivings into an idol and be curved over oneself (*incurvatum in se*).[4] Again whereas Augustine tended to write about the grace of God impersonally, Luther saw that the grace of God was his personal coming to us in Jesus Christ.[5] In a remarkable way he combined the anti-pelagian stance of Augustine, the emphasis on the role of the humanity of Christ in our redemption of St. Anselm, with the warm piety of St. Bernard to bring forth this real development of the Catholic faith.

This true christological development of Luther was taken up by Calvin who showed how the whole life of the Church must be under christological correction. "This therefore", he wrote, "is the only way of restoring and retaining true doctrine — to place Christ before the view with all his blessings that his excellency may be truly perceived".[6]

The consequences of this approach for theological training were considerable. In the Middle Ages the piety of the Church was so concentrated on sacramental grace that preaching and biblical exposition were in some areas of the Church almost unknown. Of course many did preach and expound the Bible. There were great preachers like Geiler of Strassbourg, and a whole host of mendicant friars, but preaching was regarded as an added extra. The essential saving life of Christ came to people through the Sacraments, and whole areas of the Church especially in rural areas had virtually no instruction.[7] Some priests could be theologically ignorant since their sole function was the conduct of sacramental worship. (Sometimes the ignorance was staggering. In the diocese of Gloucester some priests did not know that there were ten commandments and another thought the Lord's Prayer was so named after our lord, King Henry[8]). Of course there were many learned and pious priests and much sound theological work was being done. But with the Reformation, preaching became a necessity for all ministers and theological scholarship was geared to biblical exegesis.[9]

Of the abuses that have befallen the Church, wrote Luther, the worst is that "God's Word is not proclaimed: there is only reading and singing in the churches".[10] Calvin likened the Church to a mother who cared for her children continuously "to the end of our lives", by mediating the Word and Sacraments to them and by "discipling" them.[11] This mediation was the task of the ministry and to perform it they simply had to be steeped in the knowledge of the apostolic and prophetic witness to Christ in the Bible. "We must read the Scripture", wrote Calvin, "with the intention of finding Christ therein. If we turn aside from this end, however much trouble we take, however much time we devote to our study we shall never attain the knowledge of the truth".[12] "When we read Scripture our aim must be to be truly edified in faith and in the fear of the Lord and to be drawn to our Lord Jesus Christ, and to recognise that God has imparted Himself to us, that we may possess Him as our inheritance".[13] Consequently this was the purpose for Calvin writing the *Institutes* "to prepare and qualify students of theology for the reading of the Divine Word".[14] In Peter Barth's phrase the *Institutes* are "Calvin's forefinger pointing to Holy Scripture."

The whole point of all this biblical study for Luther and Calvin was as Calvin put it "to find Christ therein". Luther put it characteristically in his *Commentary on Romans*. "The Apostle speaks", he wrote, commenting on Romans 5: 2, "against those presumptuous persons who think they can come to God apart from Christ, as though it was sufficient for them to have believed and thus *sola fide* not through Christ, but alongside of Christ or beyond Christ, not needing to have him having once accepted the grace of justification . . . but it is necessary to have Christ always, hitherto and to eternity as the mediator of such faith . . ."[15] And later he wrote, "They therefore who interpret the Gospel as something else than good news do not understand the Gospel. Precisely that must be said of those who have turned Gospel into law rather than interpret it as grace and who set Christ before us as a Moses."[16] As Calvin insisted there is one covenant and it is a covenant of grace.[17] As soon as this emphasis is departed from troubles in the Church arise like the pelagianism and legalism both in the Mediaeval Church and in Scholastic Calvinism with its emphasis on two covenants — of works and of grace.

II

From the vantage point of the Incarnation and the cost of our redemption the whole life of man can be seen to be under grace and therefore the whole life of the Church must be controlled by this fact, and theological teaching if it is to show the truth of the Gospel must reflect this. Two points of the greatest moment arise. First the purpose of the Church is not in any way to point to itself but to reflect the glory of God in the face of Jesus Christ. Its sole message is this grace of God in Christ and what this means to mankind in all its need. (Alas, to those outside the Church what seems to come across most strongly is the Church as the upholder of the *mores* of the community or the agent of self fulfilment, not as the reflector of the character of God who stood on the side of the enemy, the outcast and the oppressed). Its works of compassion are

E

again to reflect just this, for the biblical message highlights the fact of God's concern for those who are helpless and without rights. Again in its worship, from the vantage point of the Incarnation, Christ is the true worshipper and the one sacrifice, the high priest and the offering. We, as it were, must participate in his true worship and self offering. Hence the Sacraments, and particularly the Eucharist, should be the characteristic worship of the Church as there the focus of attention is always on Christ, the "one sufficient sacrifice, oblation and satisfaction".

Secondly, justification by grace alone entails the unity of the Church and indeed is the only basis for it.[18] "Why did Christ come" asked Calvin in his great commentary on the Hebrews, "but to gather us all together in one from this dispersion in which we are now wandering. Therefore the nearer his coming is, the more we must bend our efforts that the scattered may be brought together and united that there may be one fold and one shepherd".[19] Sin is always divisive, and it was the purpose of God in forgiving sin to restore unity to a divided world. In the light of the passion of Christ we have to accept each other because we have been accepted by Christ, not because we are acceptable even to each other. We are, as Luther put it, *simul iustus et peccator*. The fact that sin divides us has to be taken seriously. But what is more important and what has to be taken more seriously is the fact that we have been accepted, by grace only, through Jesus Christ. The Gospel is about this reconciling action of Christ, and therefore the Church in order to reflect this action must show to a world so seriously divided as ours, a reconciled and reconciling family. This aspect comes out so clearly in the apostolic witness to Christ in holy Scripture. It is hard to think of a place where the unity of the Church is not spelt out as a consequence of the death of Christ. John tells how the death of Christ is to gather into one the children of God who are scattered abroad (11:51-53). The second chapter of Ephesians expounds how the death of Christ made peace between Jews and Gentiles; Colossians (2:12-3:11) insists that in our Baptism into Christ's Death and Resurrection racial barriers between Jews and Greeks, religious barriers between the Jewish circumcised and non-Jewish uncircumcised Christians, cultural barriers between Greeks and barbarians, social barriers between bond and free, have no place at all, but deny the reality of our Baptism. So the unity of the Church is not an optional extra for those who are gregariously inclined, but something that is an essential consequence of our understanding of the grace of God in Christ. Too often unity is thought of as being between people who are alike. But viewed from the vantage point of the cross it is about the reconciliation of people who are different, but who have glimpsed the fact that they are the ones for whom Christ died. There can be neither talk of accepting each other on conditions — for Christ has accepted us all unconditionally, nor talk of a union of the lowest common denominator of belief — for that is seeing it merely as a unity of those who are alike. Because it is based on the mystery of redemption then the only way forward is together to seek the fulness of the Faith. And this as St. Anselm has so clearly shown leads to deeper faith — faith, the understanding of this faith, deeper faith.[20]

III

This has a significant bearing on theological education in an ecumenical setting. The Gospel is so rich that no one Christian tradition sees it in its fulness. Indeed even altogether it is difficult to believe that they exhibit the fulness of the Faith. But if Churches (just as individuals) begin from the fact that they are accepted by Christ by grace alone, and therefore they must accept each other and if as a consequence they realise that together they are called to seek the fulness of the faith then a Faculty of Theology brought together on these premises is extremely rewarding. Its task is the common reflection upon the mystery of the Word made flesh, of the cost of our redemption, of the working out of this in the worship, witness and common life of the Church and of its significance for all the life of mankind.

I have experienced a United Faculty of Theology in Melbourne consisting of Anglicans, Jesuits and the Uniting Church (former Congregationalists, Methodists and Presbyterians) and it was very enriching. Because in this situation it is a federation of Theological Colleges, there was a great increase in our resources. Overnight the library doubled in size and was greatly enriched in quality. Experts could be called on to teach in many different theological fields. For example in Church History there were three specialists in Patristics, there was a specialist in the relations between the Eastern and Western Church, another in the theology of St. Thomas, another on the Catholic Church in the 19th Century, another on modern Anglicanism. This meant that I could give my full attention to Reformation studies. From the students' point of view it meant that they were exposed to a subject from "the inside" as it were. They could no longer consider Thomism as arid if the one who was teaching it clearly showed it as a way of viewing the Gospel. Catholic students, often for the first time, came to see Luther and Calvin as men passionately concerned with the grace of Christ in harmony with the early Fathers of the Church. One of the most exciting moments in my life as a teacher has been the way in which so many Catholics responded to this approach.

Perhaps most important was the beginning of the integration of worship and theology. All true theology must end in adoration, as expressed so movingly in many of the works of Anselm where his theological reflection merges imperceptibly into prayer. This should especially be true in the Reformed tradition centred as it is on the grace of God in Christ, but frequently this is not the case, and nowhere has this broken down more than in sacramental worship. We talk so much about the right theology of the Sacraments, about the inseparability of Word and Sacrament, of the high place they should have in the Church, yet how many of us have let the Sacraments build our devotion to Christ? There is clearly no better way for undercutting the Pelagianism that is so common in our worship than eucharistic worship for there we are taken away from our worship and our feelings to Christ's offering, his obedience and his love. One of the most helpful things in the United Faculty of Theology has been the way in which Catholic and Anglican emphasis on the Eucharist both in theology and in practice has enabled those not coming from this tradition to deepen their own piety from this style of devotion. In fact the emphasis which these two groups put upon spiritual formation has stirred up the Uniting Church members into doing far more in this area for its own students. Now we have frequent eucharistic worship, deeper Bible studies and retreats for helping build the spiritual dimension to life, and this is integrated with and partly flows from an emphasis on liturgy and the theology and history of worship in the teaching syllabus. On their parts Catholics and Anglicans have gained by incorporating biblical study into their worship, and have been forced to reflect upon many of the issues raised by the Reformation.

In an ideal ecumenical Faculty there should be representatives of the Orthodox Church to expound the christology of the Greek

Fathers, of the Lutherans to explore in depth the meaning of *sola gratia*, and of the Baptists or other gathered churches to help us understand their insights. This does not mean they are all equally true or of equal value. But starting from the standpoint of trinitarian theology and being committed together to seek the fulness of the Faith one is asking a quite different question — namely how is the faith and worship of the whole Catholic Church deepened as it reflects together on the mystery of the glory of God in the face of Jesus Christ. For those in the Reformation tradition, the centrality of justification *sola gratia per Iesum Christum Dominum nostrum* gives one an immense freedom in the life of faith. One realises, as it is all of grace, that one is defended by the Faith rather than a defender of it; that one's fellow Christians of other traditions are saved by grace just as much as those who have spelt out the doctrine creedally, important as that is to do. For spelling it out however correctly in itself does not save one. To think so, as Cranmer so astutely remarked, is to run the danger of making faith into a work.[21] What the formulating of it can do is to lead to a deeper understanding and that in turn to a deepening of faith. This deeper understanding and faith is then a much better instrument to handle sensitively the insights of one's fellow Christians and to help them deepen their faith as together one reflects upon the nature of and adores the Blessed Trinity who surrounds our whole life with grace.

NOTES

1. *Luther and Erasmus*, (Library of Christian Classics), p.333.
2. Luther, *On the Liberty of a Christian man*, Luther's Works, American Edition, 31:345.
3. Luther, *Christmas postil* 1955 and *Advent postil* 1529 quoted in G. Aulen, *Reformation and Catholicity*, (Oliver and Boyd 1959), p.83.
4. Luther *Commentary on Romans* 8.3 See E.G. Rupp, *The Righteousness of God* (1953), p.165.
5. See I.D.K. Siggins *Martin Luther's doctrine of Christ* p.248, and references 2 above, and 16 below.
6. Calvin, *Commentary on Colossians*, 1:12.
7. In Elizabethan times Puritans constantly complained about the lack of Christian knowledge and strove to send preachers "to the dark corners of the land".

8. These examples come from the Diocese of Gloucester, during Bishop Hooper's first visitation.

9. Hence Luther's attack on the dependence upon Aristotle in many Mediaeval Faculties of Theology, or Calvin's attack on the "Sophists".

10. Luther, *Tischreden*, (Table Talk), Vol. 4:62.

11. Calvin, *Institutes* 4. 1. 4, 5.

12. Calvin, *Commentary on John* 5:39.

13. Calvin quoted W. Niesel, *The Theology of Calvin*, p.27.

14. Calvin, *Institutes*, Preface.

15. Luther, *Commentary on Romans* on 5:2.

16. Luther, *Commentary on Romans* on 7:5, 6.

17. Calvin, *Institutes* 2:10:1 to 6; and James Torrance "Covenant or Contract", *Scottish Journal of Theology*, 1970. p.51

18. Lesslie Newbigin, *The Reunion of the Church*, 2nd Edit., Introduction.

19. Calvin, *Commentary on Hebrews*, 10:25.

20. John McIntyre, *St Anselm and his critics*, p.26.

21. Cranmer, *Homily on Salvation*, Works (Parker Society) 1:129-30.

6
Theological education in a World perspective

LESSLIE NEWBIGIN

Bishop Lesslie Newbigin was involved in the work of the Theological Education Fund (TEF) of the World Council of Churches (WCC). He served the Church of South India, as it became, for many years before returning to lecture at the Selly Oak Colleges in Birmingham, from where he has just retired.

The TEF had its roots in the World Mission Conference at Tambaram in 1938, which drew attention to the neglect of ministerial training in the "younger Churches". Finally launched in 1958, its staff were entrusted with the task of assisting roughly twenty centres of theological education in the "Third World" to come up to the standards of the best Theological Faculties of Europe and North America, plus improving libraries and stimulating the production of theological textbooks in the major non-European languages.

By 1978 the task was in substance accomplished, and the WCC had the courage to disband the TEF and create a new Programme for Theological Education (PTE), which will provide a worldwide forum for the exchange of experience in the whole area of ministerial formation.

However the work of TEF raised basic questions. Were the standards of western Theological Colleges really the best? Were they in any case appropriate for the needs of the Third World? Even — most challenging of all — did western Colleges really provide the kind of theological education needed by the Churches in the West themselves?

These searching questions may be grouped under three heads:
1. Questions about structure (sociological)
2. Questions about method (pedagogical)
3. Questions about content (theological)

In a paper given to the Conference of the staffs of the Church of England Theological Colleges on 3 January 1978, Bishop Newbigin looked at these three types of questions, first as they arose during the work of TEF; and second, as they perhaps confront us now in the smaller British scene. What follows is reprinted by kind permission of the Churchman.

I

Questions of structure

(a) The life-span of the TEF has been within the period of decolonization, and it is well known that during this period the searching questions of men like Roland Allen — brushed aside in the heyday of colonialism — are being raised afresh. The patterns of ministry, and therefore of ministerial formation, introduced by the western missions are now seen to have been the imposition of a style of leadership foreign to the cultures in which the Church was being planted. The rapidly growing Churches of today are those which rely on more indigenous patterns of leadership and of leadership training. Leaders in evangelism are "thrown up" from among the ordinary rank and file of these Churches. Their training happens in and through the exercise of their gifts of leadership in the situations to which they belong. The style of leadership envisaged in our western-style Theological Seminaries can only exist in a colonial situation where there are large foreign funds to support it. The point has been well put by F. Ross Kinsler of the staff of PTE in a recent paper:

> Leaders are not formed by educational institutions; pastors
> and elders cannot expect to attain the qualities of genuine
> church leaders by "going to seminary". Schools can
> contribute to the personal and intellectual growth of their
> pupils, but leadership development takes place in society, in
> the group, in the life of the church. In recent years schools
> and seminaries have tried to provide more of an environment
> for integral development, with simulation and field
> experience, but these are by and large sporadic and pale
> imitations of real life. And the socialization process of these

> institutions can be completely irrelevant or discontinuous or
> even negative as regards leadership in the churches . . .
> Seminaries withdraw their students (physically and socially)
> from the very context and processes where leadership can
> best be formed.

(b) It has been seen that the standard type of Seminary training tends to create a professional *elite* separated from the ordinary membership. A Theological Seminary is seen as a sort of Sandhurst where an officer-class is trained, thus creating a chasm between "clergy" and "other ranks". The style of training in the Church (it is held) ought to be more akin to that of a "citizen army": something which is available to all, which is not confined to one initial period, which continues all through life as members show growing capacity to profit by training and to exercise wider leadership.

(c) This line of criticism leads to the further point that the standard type of Seminary training aligns the leadership of the Church with the privileged elements in society instead of with the poor and the marginal. It thus serves to perpetuate an improper alliance between the Churches and the ruling classes in society.

Questions of method

(a) Theological education of the traditional type inevitably comes into the target area of the whole contemporary attack upon formal education associated with such names as Paulo Freire and Ivan Illich. There is a growing questioning of the assumption that education really happens in the formalized structure of the classroom. I do not attempt to enlarge upon this, for the arguments are well known.

(b) Critics point to the contrast between the methods employed in the training of the ministry and those used in the preparation of men and women for comparable professions: law, business and medicine. Law Schools — it is said — train men through the study of concrete cases and are less and less interested in general courses on the principles of law. Business Schools similarly work almost entirely through concrete projects. Medical Schools regard the "pre-clinical" years, when general theory is taught, as simply introductory to the essential training which is given in the teaching hospital. By contrast, ministerial formation still relies almost entirely on what might be called the ministerial equivalent of the "pre-clinical years".

(c) As the work of TEF went forward, more and more insistent questions were raised about the relation of what was being taught to the living context in which the Churches concerned had to give their witness. The familiar words "indigenization" and "acculturation" were found unsatisfactory because in practice they always led to a search for alliances in the conservative and backward-looking elements in society. What was needed (it was seen) was a style of ministerial training which was related to the actual and ever-changing context, which includes of course all the usual tensions between conservative and radical elements in society. Hence the horrendous word "contextualization" was born. The word is unattractive, but the thing sought for is essential. Ministry must be trained in a way which relates the Gospel to the real issues of obedience which the Church faces in this particular time and place. One of the key questions which the TEF had to face was that of the language of theology. At the beginning it was assumed that only institutions which used English or another European language could be regarded as qualifying for help, since "vernacular" training was bound to be on a "lower" level. It has taken twenty years of struggle to convince church leaders that men trained in the mother-tongue of their Church may be equipped to engage in an encounter with their culture at least as competent as those trained in English, even if they are unable to devote their primary attention to the latest scores in the ongoing battles between the various theological schools in Europe.

Questions of content

This has already brought me to the third, and most persistent criticism which has developed during the twenty years of the TEF's operations: the criticism, namely, that theology has come to the Churches of the Third World in such an intimate relation with western culture that one could not have the one without the other. It is a plain fact that if a theological student in Asia or Africa is to read with any real understanding any of the great classics of modern theology, he must be required first of all to undergo a full introduction to the whole tradition of western thought: its origins in Greek philosophy, its development in the Middle Ages, the significance of the Reformation, the Renaissance, the Enlightenment and the Industrial Revolution. There is at present a lively interest in "Third World theologies". In our supermarket culture a few new varieties on the shelf are always interesting!

But, of course, these theologies are all written in English, by men and women who have undergone many years of acculturation into western patterns of thought, and whose theology is heavily dependent on European models. "Liberation theology", for example, obviously depends heavily on Marxism. This is in no sense a criticism: matters could not be otherwise, if theology is to be done in western languages. But, of course, there is a vast amount of theology being done all the time of which western Christians must remain ignorant, because it is done in the language and thought-forms of the native culture. The Tamil language, which has a religious and philosophical literature far more ancient than any western language, is also the vehicle of a continuing stream of Christian writing hardly any of which is ever put into English. A contemporary Christian Tamil scholar and poet — in a recent article on the great Christian poet of the nineteenth century, Krishna Pillai — has remarked that it is a matter for thankfulness to God that Krishna Pillai never learned English. He was able to give his whole heart and soul to the task of interpreting Christ to his own Tamil people in poetry which ranks among the finest in the language. A style of ministerial formation which assumes that "advanced" theological training must be in a European language will exclude itself from what is most creative in the contemporary encounter of the Gospel with the cultures of the Third World.

If we set the experience of the TEF in broad historical terms, we may see it as reflecting in a tiny mirror the larger movement of our time — the movement from the first stage to the second stage of decolonization. In the first stage, the invaded culture masters the invading culture and uses its models (intellectual, juridical, political) to expel the invader. In the second stage, there is a return to the original roots of culture and the effort to find the basis for a new independence. The TEF has been an instrument to enable Churches of the Third World to come through the first stage, to develop a leadership which has fully mastered the theology which the western world brought to them. Apart from the work of TEF it is difficult to see how the present generation of outstanding Third World theologians could have developed. Now we move to the second stage. Here there is no place for the idea of "lifting" Third World theology to the level of the older Churches. Here we need to create a new type of forum in which we learn together, and from one another, how to develop styles of ministerial formation which will help the Churches in all our varying cultural situations to bring about a real encounter between the Gospel and the contemporary world. This is what the PTE exists to become.

At this point, therefore, I move to the second part of my paper to ask (and the questions must be very tentative) whether there are lessons to be learned from the experience of TEF which may be worthy of attention in the Theological Colleges and Faculties of this country.

II

Questions of structure

Must we not face the fact in this country also that the model of ministry as a full-time salaried professional group, analogous to the doctors and the lawyers, is a legacy from a period of history which has now passed? We know, in fact, that it has already broken down. We are not happy with the spectacle of aged clerics running round three or four parishes on a Sunday morning to administer Sacraments to congregations of which they are not a living part. I know that we are trying to remedy the situation by the development of non-stipendiary ministries[1] to relieve the salaried clergy of part of this load. I am wholly in favour of this. But would not a sound theology of the ministry lead us to reverse the roles as they are normally understood, to see these non-stipendiaries as the normal ministry, and the salaried clergy as auxiliaries? Would it not be in accordance both with Scripture and with our real situation if (at least in many of our scattered parishes) it was a local and respected elder of the local congregation who normally presided at the eucharist, and a full-time salaried person who would be his auxiliary both to supplement his teaching ministry and also to assist him in the continuing process of leadership-development?

I am certainly not implying a total rejection of present patterns — which would be absurd and destructive — but development in the ways I have suggested, which would include the following:

(a) Flexibility in patterns with room both for the salaried full-time and for the non-salaried part-time minister. (It is important, in this respect, that St Paul, by both claiming the right of support and refusing to exercise it has providentially left the door open both ways for the succeeding generations. It is impossible on scriptural grounds either to exclude a salaried ministry, or to demand that it shall be the only norm.)

(b) Development of a salaried ministry which is primarily concentrated on the development of local "indigenous" leadership in each congregation.

(c) Acceptance of the fact that the *normal* local leadership would be that of non-salaried members of the congregation.

(d) Willingness to learn from such rapidly growing bodies as the Pentecostals about the way in which Christian leadership can be developed in the living situation. This would not necessarily mean that we have the same criteria of leadership. With (perhaps) a more sophisticated understanding of the ministry of the Church to the public sectors of society and to those who hold specialized positions in the ordering of these sectors, we might wish to use other criteria of fitness for leadership and other models of training than the Pentecostals. But we would be willing to learn from the basic pattern of leadership-development "on the job". (I am assuming here that we are planning for our contemporary type of urban society in which the private sector is sharply separated in the lives of most people from the public sector.)

(e) In using the word "leadership", I am obviously distancing myself from the currently fasionable attack on *elites*. (I have sometimes thought of founding a society for the encouragement of *elites*!) I fully recognize the justice of this attack. But I think it is one of the illusions of our time that the participation of the whole body comes about otherwise than by the exercise of gifts of leadership. There are types of leadership which cause individual initiative to wither. True leadership seeks it out and encourages it. But "leadership" within the Christian vocabulary can only mean that leadership which Jesus exercises when he calls his disciples to follow him on the way that goes to the cross.

(f) If these lines of thinking were followed, it would mean that the normal customer for what we offer in the way of ministerial training would not be a young man (or woman) at the beginning of a professional career, but someone of mature Christian experience who is proving himself in actual situations to have the kind of capacity for leadership (defined in the sense of the previous paragraph) which is appropriate to the life of Christ's people.

Questions of method

The implications of what I am saying would — I think — lead to a shift in our styles of ministerial formation which would bring them nearer to the patterns suggested in the training of lawyers and doctors. A much larger place would be given than is now common to the study of particular cases in which the issues for Christian faith and obedience can be teased out, discussed, and related to the great themes of the Bible and of the classical Christian tradition. I do not think that this can ever be the *only* way in which theology is taught, but I think it could and should have a larger place than at present. Here, however, I would want to enter two *caveats*.

(a) I am not advocating the sort of "contextualization" which in effect eliminates the text in favour of the context. The statement that "real theology arises out of concrete situations" can be taken to mean that one arrives at a true theology by purely inductive processes: studying the world in order to find out "what God is doing". In that case it parts company completely from the Christian faith, which depends upon a unique revelation which can never be replaced by any other sort of communication. The end of "contextuality" in that (false) sense is either some sort of paganism, or else some sort of crusading moralism. The gospel is not discovered by analysing the situation. The true sense in which we should say that theology must be contextual is that we can know God as he has revealed himself to us in Jesus Christ only as we are continuously engaged as his disciples in the actual context of secular affairs in which God has placed us, and that a theology divorced from such discipleship will be a false theology.

(b) I am also disinclined to endorse without qualification the phrase constantly repeated by the theologians of liberation that "true theology is a reflection on praxis". It is certainly true that there can be no authentic theology which is not part of a life of faith, worship and obedience within the believing community. These are the conditions for a true contextualization of theology. What must be rejected is the idea that one begins with praxis based upon a Marxist analysis of the situation and then proceeds to reflect theologically upon it. It seems to me that some of the exponents of liberation theology, in their justified rejection of the philosophical idealism which has so often formed the (unacknowledged) presupposition of traditional theology, have swallowed uncritically the Marxist idea that all science depends upon class-orientation. In fact, of course, the doctrine that in order to evaluate a statement one must first ask "Whose interest does it serve?" has not been uniformly applied in Marxist theory. Michael

Polanyi has discussed this point in several of his writings. To summarize the matter briefly: Marx and Engels seem to have accepted nineteenth-century physics, chemistry and mathematics as giving a true account of reality irrespective of the class-orientation of the scientists. Consequently these sciences have been allowed to develop in the Soviet Union without ideological control by the party. Human sciences, such as economics and sociology, have never been given such autonomy. The borderline case of biology has been the subject of a well-known effort at ideological control (under the leadership of Lysenko) with disastrous results. The effort has had to be abandoned. It seems to me that there are no good reasons for trying to do for theology what has never been attempted in respect of the natural sciences and has proved disastrous in respect of biology.

Having made these negative statements I would go on to affirm that true theology can be done only in a community which is committed to faithful discipleship, including both worship and practical obedience. It is this conviction which has led to efforts to involve theological students in action programmes of various kinds. The most impressive of these known to me are those in operation at the Tamilnadu Theological Seminary, Madurai, South India.

But, as has been pointed out, there is an element of artificiality in these programmes. Having withdrawn students from their normal secular activities into a residential community, you then try to reinvolve them as a community in secular situations. There does seem to be a case for saying that the norm for theological training should be the extension type of programme. Here the theological training runs concurrently with the secular engagement, and there seems to be more possibility of an authentic "contextuality", since the students will be coming to their theological reading and discussion with their minds already fully involved in secular situations where ordinary Christians have to find and do the will of God from day to day. There is also, it seems to me, a much greater possibility that the theology learned in such a way will be a genuinely missionary theology: a theology concerned with the world and God's purpose in it, not just with the Church. If this kind of ministerial formation were the norm, there would have to be specialist training — for example — for industrial mission; the trainees would themselves be hammering out their understanding of the Gospel in the midst of their actual wrestling with the powers at work in industry, in public administration, in the professions and in the media.

And this brings me to my third section.

Questions of content

Here the possible issues for discussion are so vast that I can only skirt the edges of them. If a "world perspective" has anything to contribute to the reshaping of theological training in this country, I suggest that it may be chiefly at the point of helping us to be aware of the unexamined assumptions which underlie most of our contemporary western European theology. I believe that European theology is to a dangerous extent encapsulated within a particular culture, and that it may be the role of our partners in other areas of the world to make us aware of this.

The word "myth" is being bandied about freely at the moment, and much confusion is caused by the differing senses in which it can be used. Let me use it in a non-pejorative sense to denote the models, the images, the patterns through which a whole community grasps and makes sense of its experience. In this broad sense there is no sharp break between the models used by science to make intelligible the structure of the molecule or the gene, and the models used by ordinary people to make sense of their experiences of joy and sorrow, pain and comfort, guilt and death. In fact we usually use the word "myth" to describe the models used by other people, for the simple reason that we are normally no more aware of our own "myths" than I am of the curvature of the lens in my spectacles. We do not "see" our own myths; we see by means of them, and we normally take it for granted that we are seeing things as they really are.

The most powerful myth of our culture is that which is usually described as the "modern scientific world view", in contrast to the world view which preceded it. The study of the exact nature of the change which took place, mainly during the eighteenth century, in the way in which western European man understood his world is a fascinating one. It is perhaps especially important at the present time when this "modern" view shows many signs of disintegrating. The point, however, is that this view — though it has been and still is enormously influential — is still only one of the possible ways of grasping the totality of human experience. My criticism of much contemporary theology is that it so often fails to recognize this. I find it very interesting, for example, that such a brilliant and sensitive expositor of the Christian Faith as Hans Kung can write that the theologians of the other great world Religions will have to develop a "modern scientific theology" before there can be real dialogue among the world Religions. In contrast to such a view, I would want to assert that the great service which the ecumenical movement can do for us is to confront us with ways of affirming the Christian Faith which are formed by other cultures than our own. It is only with this help that we shall be able to subject our own cultural "myth" to examination in the light of the Gospel. Without this ecumenical correction we are always tempted to judge the Gospel in the light of our myth; the real task of ecumenical theology will be to learn how to use the different myths of different cultures to communicate a Gospel which transcends them all.

In fact we are still far from such a truly ecumenical theology because we have created a situation in which the only languages in which the ecumenical conversation can be conducted are the languages of western Europe, and consequently the only theologians of the Third World who can play a real part in the conversation are those who have been co-opted into the dominant European culture with its accepted myths and models. Nevertheless the voice of protest is coming through. I am thinking of the witness of those churches which are the contemporary growing edge of Christendom — the Pentecostals and the African independent Churches. Their way of doing theology is — I am convinced — bound to become a more and more powerful critique of those which are dominant in this country. I am sure, for example, that the extreme nervousness and circumspection with which English theologians of today approach the subject of the Resurrection of Jesus from the dead will eventually have to meet the challenge of these vigorously growing communities of believers for whom it is precisely the Resurrection which is the very heart of their Gospel.

The ultimate commitment of the Christian theologian is to the biblical myth. Yet he is also a man of his own culture and his whole way of thinking is shaped by the myths of that culture. He cannot absolutize his own cultural myth, and from within it judge the biblical; that is, it seems to me, the temptation of contemporary European theology. His task — and it is the unending task of a missionary theology — is to open his whole being to the biblical myth in such a way that his own myth is placed in its light, and then

F

to find ways in which the biblical myth can be expressed in terms which use the form of the cultural myth without being controlled by it. But this, I would claim, can only be done if he is continuously open to the witness of Christians in other cultures who are seeking to practice the same kind of theology. In fact, as I have argued in another place at some length,[2] I believe that a true theology can only be done in a triangular field of which the three points are: (a) Obedient discipleship within the Christian community and governed by the tradition of which the Scriptures are the primary embodiment; (b) Openness to the witness of Christians in other cultural situations as they seek to communicate the Gospel in the models of their cultures; (c) Openness to the culture within which the theologian has to live out his discipleship.

One practical implication of this, it seems to me, is that the task of theological training cannot be simply handed over to the Universities. It is the task of the Church, and the Church must take the responsibility. But, provided the proper independence is maintained on both sides, the opportunity to do theology in a university setting is something which must be welcomed. In this connection I am impressed by the possibilities contained in the development of the Cambridge Federation of Theological Colleges. Here there is an impressive recognition of the need to do theology in the context of the confessing and worshipping Church, and at the same time a very open involvement in the work of a University Faculty which is not committed to this context. This seems to me to provide the opportunity for real dialogue between the Gospel and our culture. The test will come, of course, when the Christian theologian has to raise questions about the very presuppositions upon which the University Faculty operates. Certainly an alert Church will not be beguiled into thinking that a flourishing University Department of Religious Studies is any kind of substitute for a centre for Christian theology.

The newly created Programme for Theological Education of the World Council of Churches provides a forum in which the kind of inter-cultural sharing of experience in theological training which I have indicated can take place. I hope and believe that the initiative taken by the British Council of Churches to provide for vigorous British participation in this will be effective.

NOTES

1. This refers to Episcopal clergy who take other employment and serve their congregations in their spare time.
2. *Christ and the Cultures*, Scottish Journal of Theology, Vol 31, 1978 pP.1-32

7

Athens and Jerusalem[1]

HERBERT A. KERRIGAN

I

Traditionally the relationship between the Universities and the Church in Scotland has been a close, happy and mutually respectful affair. The normal course for the ministry included a general education, usually in Arts, provided by the University prior to the undertaking of theological studies. Thus the minister had the general liberal education offered by the University before embarking on his subsequent course which might be provided by that body or by a college under the direction of a particular branch of the Church. The Church greatly influenced the Universities but there are few examples in their mutual history of the Church dominating the Universities or of stifling their general academic growth or of limiting academic freedom. Gradually Church Colleges as such became phased out and in each of the ancient Scottish Universities there came into being Theological Colleges in name which were in fact simply part of the Universities with varying methods of appointment of staff.

The critical appointments have long been regarded as those to Professorships within the Faculties of Divinity because of the particular responsibility which the individual professor bears for the manner in which his subject is taught, the interpretation of the regulations about the scope of his subject (which is generally a matter for himself, subject to the University's general surveillance), the development of research in his area of interest and the eventual clarification and re-definition of his and his subject's role within the Faculty. Few would doubt the influence which a particular professor could bring to bear in so interpreting his subject, leaving his Chair with a distinctive reputation within the tradition of the College in which he functioned. Many can recall variations in the approach to the same subject amongst the holders of like Chairs which led to greater general academic stimulation or the development of a particular tradition within one of the Colleges by the succession of incumbents.

The manner of appointment was often dependent upon the history of the Chair and its location. In Aberdeen the Synod made the appointment although there were representatives of the Senatus of the University of Aberdeen involved in the nomination. Certain other Chairs were within the gift of the Crown where the Secretary of State would advise a nomination after private consultation with the Church and the particular University. In the University of Glasgow certain appointments were made by the University Court after consultation with the Church on an informal basis, and the Curators of Patronage in the University of Edinburgh adopted a similar practice before appointing. In the pre-Union Colleges of the United Free Church of Scotland the appointments were made by the General Assembly, nomination having ocurred by Presbyteries and Synods to theological chairs within the Scottish Universities. However the "Church Chairs" (i.e. those of the former United Free Church of Scotland) continued to be in the gift of the General Assembly where the Church's Board of Nomination alone nominates to the General Assembly (or Commission) which makes the appointment. Thereafter the local Presbytery ordains and/or inducts to the appointment.

II

Changes after 1932. After the Union of 1929 there was a certain confusion which required to be regularised by the Universities (Scotland) Act 1932 which Act (as amended by the Universities (Scotland) Act 1966) is still in force.

The University Court became the uniform body for appointments. Thus in many cases the body making the appointment was unaltered whilst the Crown, the General Assembly, Synod of Aberdeen and the Curators of Patronage in Edinburgh all lost their power of appointment!

The power of nomination passed to Boards of Nomination of representatives of both University Court and the General Assembly in equal numbers.

In 1950 Draft Agreements between the various University Courts and the General Assembly were placed before the Assembly and these still stand subject to the 1966 Act which gave the University Court of each of the Scottish Universities power to alter the Ordinances in consultation with the Church.

The present procedure for appointment. It is this:—
1. Upon a vacancy in a Church Chair the nomination is to and the appointment by the General Assembly as outlined above.
2. Upon a vacancy in a University Chair the nomination is by a Board comprising half representatives of the particular University Court and representatives appointed by the General Assembly.
3. The nomination to a University Chair must be by two thirds of the Board who must intimate their nomination within twelve months of the vacancy.
4. If no such intimation is made the University Court can make the appointment without reference to the Board.

The other change introduced by the 1932 Act. Perhaps the other most significant change in the 1932 Act was the provision in section 5 that no principal, professor, regent, master or other office bearer in any University or College in Scotland could make and subscribe the acknowledgement or declaration in the Act for securing the Protestant religion and Presbyterian Church Government.

This provision was clearly necessary to rid the Universities and Colleges of the old Test Act provisions which were rightly regarded by many as anathema. The other provisions of the Act gave the Church a high degree of protection from the appointment of those considered to be unsuitable for holding office as professors in Faculties of Divinity.

It did however open the way for the appointment of those who were not Presbyterian but who might be acceptable teachers within the Faculties. There were however few professorial appointments where the provision had any significance until the events of 1979. The climate of 1932 and the supervening years was such that appointments were generally of Presbyterians or of those of a tradition close to Presbyterianism and generally within the Reformed family of Churches.

The manner of exercising appointments. Close scrutiny of the ordinances currently in force reveals differences in approach to nomination which are but slight in terms of the written word. What is however of greater significance is the amplification of the regulations in the practice of the various Universities in sounding out opinion prior to making an appointment. It is true however that there is variance in the practice of e.g. the University of Aberdeen's Christ's College as opposed to the situation in the University of Edinburgh's New College, but the most significant feature in my view is the manner of exercising the function of nomination which occurs, and not the system by itself. This is exemplified in the events of 1979.

III

The events of 1979. In June 1979 the University Court of the University of Edinburgh appointed a Roman Catholic to the Thomas Chalmers Chair which had hitherto been held by a succession of distinguished Presbyterian theologians. This was the first such appointment. It caused a storm of protest within the Church of Scotland. This was not directed personally at the appointee who was caught in the midst of the controversy. The protest was directed at those who made the nomination. The nomination was made in accordance with the procedures outlined above. There was a Board of Nomination of twelve, six of whom had been appointed to the Board by the General Assembly's appropriate committee. The other six were representatives of the University Court but included a high number who were in fact ministers of the Church of Scotland and the others also had some connection with the Church of Scotland it is believed. Thus the end result was not the product of a papist plot but the judgement of a group of individuals who had some tangible connection with the Church of Scotland.

I first learned of the possibility of such an appointment early in the General Assembly and raised the matter by way of motion when the appropriate Committee was reporting. This motion expressed the hope that a Reformed theologian would be appointed but was lost in the mists of whether a Reformed or reformed theologian was too narrow a definition and in what seemed the general obscurity of the whole question. At that stage not even Dr. Morris of Glasgow Cathedral, who was presenting the Report, had an indication of what the Sub Committee acting under the General Assembly's authority was doing. An attempt by a member of the Sub Committee to have my motion declared out of order was repelled and thus the point had been raised. Over the week investigative journalism led one to the view that there was possibly some substance in the rumours circulating about the appointment and the matter came before the Assembly on the Closing Day with the recall of the Committee.

When the matter was raised on that day in answer to a question by me it was made clear that the decision on the nomination was a *fait accompli* and had been for some time prior to the Assembly. Due to the question of confidentiality no information was given as to the name of the nominee. The Assembly, despite various attempts to divert it from this course made it clear that a nomination of a Roman Catholic Theologian was not acceptable and asked the University Court not to make such an appointment.

The point however was that at least two (and there is no reason to suppose it was more) of the Church Nominees agreed to the appointment in the initial stages of the Board's deliberation, and dissent by the others would have been ineffective. Perhaps the candidates were few from the traditional background, or the appointee so outstandingly well qualified for the appointment that the choice was irresistible. Be that as it may, the threatened appointment led to an unprecedented expression of disapproval of the Assembly's Committee's acting. One felt sorry for those who, as Dr. Roy Sanderson put it, were fettered with a decision which in conscience they may not have agreed with but could not disclaim; yet it is surprising that those who did misjudge the Church's mind have not had the courage to own up to this.

IV

Academic freedom. The University of Edinburgh considered that it had to accept the nomination and one can well understand the Court's position in this regard. In a statement the Court pointed out that it had to be alive to academic freedom and affirmed that its Faculty of Divinity would maintain as one of its major responsibilities the commitment to the teaching and training of those preparing for the Ministry of the Church of Scotland. With these viewpoints one cannot disagree.

The problem however is this. In order to maintain true academic freedom there must be outlets for various academically worthy approaches to particular fields. One has no reason to doubt that the new incumbent will do anything other than provide an academically stimulating and worthy education for his students perhaps in a unique manner in the light of his own intellect, opportunities, experience and learning. One wonders however if the basic tradition to which he belongs is not adequately catered for in numerous Universities, Colleges and Seminaries throughout the world, whereas the Chairs in the tradition hitherto that of the Thomas Chalmers Chair are few and far between if others in fact exist. What in that situation is academic freedom?

What of the training of those for the ministry of the Church of Scotland? Is it simply a form of brainwashing to suggest that their training in Christian Dogmatics should be from one schooled in the tradition they are to profess as their life's work and witness? Will they not benefit from the greater comparative study which may call them towards the search for truth rather than the dogged acceptance of tradition? Is it not compatible with the current spirit of ecumenicity and the hope many of us have for closer future ecumenical relations? Would however ecumenical relations not have been furthered more by the appointment of one readily identified as being in the main line of his own Church's practice and dogma as evidenced by his enjoying full status and having had a continuous pastoral role within his denomination? Were not many members of the Roman Catholic Church outraged by the appointment in Edinburgh for reasons different from their Presbyterian brethren? Was it not the case, looking at the composition of the Board, that a number of those from the Divinity Faculty must have adjudged this appropriate for their needs as well as the Church representatives? Would it really be neglecting the other 75% of the students to emphasise particular needs, if such exist, of the Church of Scotland candidates?

The Church's viewpoint. There is however strong feeling, if I interpret it aright, within the Church of Scotland that the Church should accept the primary responsibility for the provision of education for the ministry within its own tradition. Perhaps embittered by the effect of the partial abrogation of responsibilities for the Christian education of children to the secular educational authorities and its results, many members of the Church are concerned about a like abrogation to the Universities.

Whilst paternalism is generally unpopular no University teacher can deny the effect he can have on fertile and receptive minds. The student approaching theological training will have had some compulsion leading to that point and towards the ministry of that be the goal. He will have a basic belief. He will have an experience either gradual or sudden. He may have made extensive preparation by earlier degree or private study, but the average undergraduate in divinity will be coming with what is hopefully a fresh and fertile mind. In those circumstances there is a clear duty on the Church to provide its candidates with teaching in all aspects grounded in its own traditions. Indeed comparative study can only benefit from a good base.

This is not to say that in the later stages of his training a candidate should not be exposed to the most rigorous challenge to his views in a therapeutic situation. I say rigorous challenge because that is what he can expect in his ministry wherever he is, but it must be a setting where he can have understanding pastoral support. This is an area which seems to me to set apart a Divinity Faculty. It is not simple the understanding of doctrine or the communication of it, but seeing its application in a pastoral setting — and this can only be taught by those who have had the like experience. In my own early days in University teaching, when I had not practised law, I realised that whilst one was able to communicate the bones of the subject the experience of practice would provide the flesh to enable the student to see more of the body of law. Perhaps the Church would wish to consider the example set by the legal profession in Scotland. Because of a dual frustration — that of the academics in considering that too much time was devoted to rote learning of subjects which required little academic approach but simply practical experience, and that of the practitioner who considered that practical subjects were inadequately taught by those of minimal experience — the diploma in legal practice is being introduced following upon the law degree as an essential prerequisite prior to embarking in practice. In some ways it seems that the Diploma in Pastoral Theology following upon the Bachelor's or Licentiate's courses is a parallel but it is not mandatory nor can time reasonably be spent on this if a candidate takes both Arts and Divinity. It would seem however that this may be one alternative to Church Colleges.

If I interpret the situation correctly there is some feeling amongst academics that the resources in terms of staff and faculties given to the Faculties of Divinity may be over generous in the light of the number of students. Whilst it has always been recognised that the Universities have a role to play in the preparation of candidates for the ministry and thereby in making resources available the Church cannot rely on that generous attitude prevailing indefinitely in the light of constant cutbacks which erode vital research and development. The availability of places for candidates who would otherwise have chosen to enter other Faculties has perhaps given the Divinity Faculties a false sense of security. I have been surprised to hear reaction from many, not opposed to the Church, who feel that the time has come for a full reappraisal of resources, and the Church must be alive to this. It would be ironic if the happenings at one University led to reappraisal and reduction in others.

The Church must be prepared to consider making financial support available to a greater degree for the training of her ministry. The case for a Church College is fully argued elsewhere, and many features seem to point to its desirability. It might however be worthwhile to consider before doing this the history of good relations between the Universities and the Church of Scotland. Also worth considering is the satisfactory nature of the concordat between the Universities and the Church providing that the interests of the Church are protected by those who represent it (or even have a dual hat to wear). The financial implications are such that in my view the concordat between Athens and Jerusalem must be maintained, Caesar allowed to have that which is his, but God's interests protected by those who serve him.

NOTE

1. The title reflects a saying of the early Christian leader Tertullian: "What is there in common between Athens and Jerusalem? What between the Academy and the Church? What between heretics and Christians?" cited in Bettenson, *Documents of the Christian Church* 2nd ed. p.8

8

Freedom and order in theological education

COLIN SINCLAIR

"I am the truth". In an upper room surrounded by his closest followers, these words were first spoken by Jesus to meet the troubled heart of a confused and doubting disciple on a night pregnant with foreboding. Today when faith is assailed on all sides, or even worse simply ignored and dismissed, these words come down to us as a charter of liberty to inspire and challenge each new generation. They set Christians gloriously free from the ghetto mentality which retreats into itself and refuses to face the demands and questions of the world around it. They are a green light to those who have worried whether the free untrammelled pursuit of truth would betray, or expose as inconsistent their loyalty to Christ. Reinforcing that part of the great commandment which calls us to love God with all our minds, they enable us to think creatively, to explore God's universe, confident that all truth revealed will be in harmony with, and will point up, the glories of Christ.

It is this dominical statement that is the legitimate basis of academic freedom. It asserts that no area of search, where truth is the object, can be barred to the Christian (except that which God has expressly forbidden in Scripture, knowing that the consequences would be destructive to personality and life), for ultimately the cosmic Lord of the Universe, the Word to whom all creation owes its origin and continued existence, is revealed as master of that particular realm also. From anyone else such claims would not only be outrageous in their extravagance but embarrassing in their obvious deceit, but there was nothing incongruous about the words of Christ, for they expressed his character.

I

What then are the implications of such a statement for theological education? First, it puts an end to all attempts to rigidly demarcate the areas of theological concern; as if God had no reference to the study of economics, but was only involved in biblical theology. If man does not live by bread alone, then economics is incomplete without a theological perspective. Of course, systematic theology has its particular subject matter, as do the related subjects studied at Theological College, but the preacher and Christian apologist then faces the challenge of relating modern astronomy to the doctrine of creation, and so on. In our age of specialisation, scholars have to sacrifice a general conspectus in order to delve into particular minutiae. The theologian stands over against all that, refusing to sacrifice the basic unity and dynamic of the whole of human life and thought, asserting instead that there is a unifying point in Christ himself.

Second, the Christian must face up to all the obstacles to Christian faith, to its legitimacy and expression. In our western world it is widely or tacitly assumed that God can be ignored without consequence and living faith is regarded as obsolescent. There have been attacks made, direct and indirect, on traditional faith both from outside and inside the Church. What is the response of theological education? If Christ is who he is, and if the Christian faith is true as it claims to be, then nothing new can be discovered which destroys faith (though it may refine it). Having said that, one is not advocating that we simply ignore as a passing phenomenon all that attacks the Church and the Gospel. That would not only be arrogance, but would disregard the humanity and worth of those who question and doubt. Rather, accepting the fact that not every criticism and question can be immediately answered, the response of theological education is to seek to get behind the attack and to attempt to find the source, the stumbling block from which such attack emerged. Of course there are some attacks which spring from illwill and antagonism, and have their roots not so much in intellectual difficulties as in unwillingness to admit the moral claims of God in Christ upon a person's life. Such questions the Christian can legitimately ignore. Where honest questions in good faith are asked the Christian must seek to give an honest answer (even if it is to confess that he is not God!). He must see if the Church's presentation of the Gospel, or its lifestyle, is in fact at odds with its calling. Indeed the question can promote a creative tension out of which the Church can grow into fresh obedience. For Christian life, being ultimately a relationship with God in Christ, is not static. It has all the wealth of potential development of any relationship between persons. Was it not a Pilgrim Father who stated with confidence that God had still more light to break forth from his Word?

Now this is both exciting and demanding, exciting because we are forced to take the unchanging truths of God, and of man, and of salvation, and to relate them reverently and relevantly to the needs, demands and perplexities of a twentieth century world. Therefore there must be given in any course of theological study a fair representation of views opposed or alternative to the Christian position. If this is not done it will mean that the Christian minister coming out to face the world can never fully hold his head up high, for there will always be that nagging doubt, that lingering question that somehow in some way he had never fully exposed his faith to the intellectual test. If Christ is the truth then we can do so humbly and yet fearlessly. Furthermore without such study the preacher will tend to be irrelevant.

Third, it follows that theological education does have a place for creativity. We are not simply called unthinkingly to regurgitate or repeat the formulas, the credal statements of an earlier generation. We cannot despise them, we cannot lay them aside and we must learn from them but we need not fear when in our thinking and understanding we are led in new directions and given new insights. Open to new ideas, we should seek to examine thoroughly the roots from which they spring, always holding fast to the truth which is our heritage and examining what is new in that light so as to work towards a new harmony.

Fourth, because academic freedom emerges from Christ himself we must say that it is not only a privilege but a great responsibility. Christ upholds the universe by his power and is the heir of all things (Heb 1:2-3). He tells us to knock at the door (Mat 7:7). This puts an end to pious sentiment, to sloppy thinking which refuses to get to grips with the matter in hand — its meaning, implications and application. Today this is the challenge of academic freedom in a world that is experientially oriented and has so often sold out hard thought for the twin gods of personal peace and affluence. It is not only a charter to think, it is a command to think and we are called one and all, whilst respecting the mystery that ultimately is God, yet to press on to think and think and think. We are not just allowed to enquire, we are called to enquire. This responsibility stands in marked contrast to so many of the ideologies and -isms with which we are increasingly familiar in our global village. Our media have made us more informed than perhaps any other age of the market cries of competing "religious" merchants with their tawdry goods. For behind the hard sell and the varied appeal quickly emerges a circumscribed outlook on life which prescribes answers and censors questions. Indoctrination, wearisome cant, stereotyped dogma — this is the name of the game.

II

Having asserted the place of academic freedom in theological education, it is not to be seen as a contradiction but rather as a qualification to say that there are in fact inevitable limits to this freedom. These limits do not arise out of theology itself but from the nature of the enquirer as a person who is finite and fallen. These two aspects while different are hard to separate.

(a) By recognising man's finiteness I do not mean that we have to resort to the acceptance of the relativism so common in our day. It would be unnatural, however, not to recognise our inability to reach an exhaustive or final statement of truth. We are not God and we require God's revelation for the truth we affirm with confidence. This revelation will never enable us to *comprehend* God but does allow us to *apprehend* him. It is not the fault of this revelation that our handling of it has a temporal quality and wears the blinkers of one age and culture.

This leads us into an issue that has troubled our Church for a century at least, the tension between academic freedom and confessional orthodoxy. We have maintained the right to liberty of thought and enquiry within the Church. Men must be honest to their convictions. Scholarship has its place. There can be no justification for obscurantism or for the clinging on to outmoded prejudices. As Marcus Dods said, "The man who refuses to face facts doesn't believe in God". So there must be an end to anything that is simply reactionary conservatism, bigoted narrow-mindedness or simply cowardly escapism.

What then is the place of confessional orthodoxy in theological education? Confessions of whatever sort are the attempt of the Church to express a general consent to the central elements of the Christian Faith as they are given by revelation of God. They recognise an authority greater than human reason (though not necessarily unreasonable), which calls for acceptance by faith. Unlike the revelation which it seeks to summarize, the confession is fallible and insufficient. But its place is retained. In the Church of Scotland, ministers verbally accept the Westminster Confession of Faith, but yet due to the Declaratory Acts framed at the end of last century are allowed liberty of conscience with regard to matters "not entering into the substance of the Faith".

What is being recognised here by a confession is man's finiteness. For in any thinking man needs a starting point. What the confession does is to say that the starting point is God and not man. Everyone starts with his basic assumptions and presuppositions and these are ultimately a matter of faith. The problem today is that the basic assumptions of the Christian and the non–Christian are worlds apart. This primary difference leads to many other disagreements. The prevailing philosophical outlook is that of naturalism, of cause and effect within a closed system. There is no place here for a supernaturalistic Christianity and correspondingly if this naturalistic outlook is meekly accepted then one's attitude to the Bible and to the person and work of Christ is bound to be less than it is meant to be. I am not wanting to dismiss the scientific approach, the concern for objectivity, the place of experimentation, hypothesis and verification as of no value. In theological study it provides a corrective to fanciful thinking. Yet what I would argue is that it is not sufficient. For there are realms where naturalistic thought will unavoidably conceal the truth of the Faith and indeed work contrary to the Gospel. To cite biblical examples: Moses in Pharoah's court, Daniel in Nebuchadnezzar's, or Saul in the school of the Pharisees, all received an excellent education by the standards of the day. But in no case was it sufficient preparation. Each had then further to embark in the school of faith or discipleship which transcended the previous categories of thought and expectation. They had to come to terms with the living God who breaks into history and controls history. The problem is that even a Theological College may lose this added dimension and theological disciplines proceed with a sterile naturalism which when exposed contradicts the Faith of the

Church, or — perhaps just as dangerous — makes that teaching appear a little unscholarly. But Christian faith is eminently reasonable within the bounds of its own presuppositions, and I would hold that these assumptions and their outworkings make better and more comprehensive sense than others currently advocated.

In Life and Work for July, 1979, T. F. Torrance, writing about the present state of education for the ministry, argues that "there is a real crisis of faith and spirituality in the Church and its ministry". He questions the high quality of academic training provided in our Colleges: "I personally do not think it is high enough, for there seems little rigorous examination of the assumptions that govern our biblical interpretation or theological teaching". His concern for the state of the Church finds its origins in "a serious decline in belief in our Theological Colleges often justified so bravely under the banner of 'academic freedom' and 'search for truth' when in point of fact most of this is trapped in obsolete subjective prejudices!" He calls for a spiritual and evangelical renaissance starting in our Theological Colleges.

(b) Man's fallenness is seen in his tendency to exclude God from his thinking. He attempts to put himself at the centre and God, if he has a place at all, is pushed to the periphery. Man glories in his self-sufficiency and would tend to exalt his reason at the expense of revelation. But this is to make a false polarisation. For on the basis of God's revelation a whole new agenda of questions arise which stretch the keenest mind and satisfy the finest intellect. So often though, men get bogged down with the preliminary questions, revelling in a theology of doubt. What is satisfactory intellectual gymnastics to the academic cuts no ice with men engrossed with the problems of life. They want not idle speculation or vain theorising but practical directions for the business of living life as it is meant to be lived (i.e. Practical Theology!). The day after Jesus said "I am the truth", Pilate sought to embroil Jesus in philosophical wrangling. "What is truth?", he asked but he received no reply for he was about to wash his hands of the answer and seal the truth within a tomb. Truth could not be bound but the answer eluded Pilate. What alarms me from my short experience of Theological College is that so often the questions discussed are those of Pilate, those posed by an onlooker to life and faith not by a traveller through it. Far from being superior questions they are simply different, and I would maintain secondary ones.

To accept Jesus' statement is to accept also that truth requires a christocentric approach. He must be our starting point and the focus of our thinking. In the teaching of a College curriculum how watertight can be Christ's exclusion from Old Testament theology and literature, for example? The question is sharpened if members of both the staff and student body engage in study without bringing their life and thought under the authority of Christ. If this approach becomes a norm then the Faculty creates a division between College and Church. For if living faith has no place in theological study then it has no right in the Church. Yet it has a central place in both. I would not wish to cut the College off from Faculty. The world of the University helps to "earth" a student's theology. I am certainly not advocating holy retreat which is unnatural, unrealistic and only serves to isolate potential ministers from the people whom they are called to work amongst. I do argue though that faith is a necessary prerequisite; that revelation from God through Jesus Christ, incarnate, crucified and risen is a basic presupposition; that prayer and a spiritual life are part of the essential equipment with which to study theology if one seeks to prepare for the ministry. Theology is not a hobby; it is not for the dilettante. It is concerned about salvation, about eternal life, and about the knowledge of God, and only thus can it throw light on the whole of human life.

III

Let me seek to draw out an underlying tension which has emerged in what has been said. Whom does the College seek to serve, the Church or the University? The answer in fact at present is both, for the College is a Church College recognised as the place of preparation for the ministry, and yet also a Faculty of the University and must therefore conform to its regulations and standards. Theoretically if this system can work there is much to be gained by such a union and in experience one cannot gainsay some of the benefits that have arisen from the *concordat*. It would be, however, naive not to recognise that there are tensions and dangers which the Church should monitor if the Colleges are to provide an adequate service for the Church of Scotland, and indeed for the wider Christian Church.

In the issues I seek to raise I am very conscious that I am speaking as a present student in a situation which is ever changing. I speak conscious of having had two very happy years at College and being very grateful for friendships with staff and students. I would not pretend to represent students or to generalise. I recognise that as a student I lack the reflective capacity of experience but seek in its place to offer the intimacy of current involvement. It seems to be impossible to exclude from the College the standards of University life in terms of the prevailing milieu. Thus I would maintain that it is easy for a desire for intellectual integrity to lapse into an idolatry of intellect. Academic prestige is then coveted and the fear of losing academic respectability becomes a governing factor. To win a reputation or even to have research published in academic circles can at times promote the study of the obscure; the overstating of a case; or a pandering to the current acclaim for novelty. All this is detrimental to theological training which must not accommodate itself to the prevailing fashions of the world. The Church is not looking primarily to the Colleges for mental ability or scholastic achievement but for men who are fitted to preach, equipped to pastor the people of God and to make known the Gospel. I would concede that in a day of Christian pluralism there is the need to state a variety of viewpoints on different issues. It is good to stimulate students to think, but there must also be a place for the affirmation and defence of the doctrines of the Church. I respect the freedom the Colleges give to pursue one's own avenue of study and the openness with which they receive a variety of outlooks. I would not like to see this replaced with a stereotyped training or move towards a more authoritarian regime but I would like to see clearer perimeters drawn on one's freedom. Is there not a certain basic instruction that needs to be given and a course of direction that needs to be set? How can the Church be bold from the pulpit if it is timid and insecure in its study? Is this not hypocrisy? Do not Schools of Religious Studies provide adequate alternative opportunities for those with an abstract interest in religion, leaving the Theological Colleges with the prime emphasis on preparing people, equipping them, for their future life-work and service? This would include nurture of the individual and specific courses of training. How true is it of our Colleges that they are oriented to this goal, concerned with the products of their training and not just the parchments they earn?

In a day when there is much talk about crisis in the Church, one element of this must be the frightening degree of ignorance among Church members of biblical truth. Let me quote again Professor Torrance: "Many young ministers whom I meet again after several years in the parish tell me that they are staggered at the basic ignorance of congregations in the basic elements of the Christian Faith. Evidently Communicants classes have often been of a rather perfunctory nature, while Sunday school and Bible class teaching are so concerned to be 'with it' that they are often quite devoid of the evangelical substance of the Christian message." Consequently theological students may embark upon a course of study with very little background from which to test the various critical views presented by the Colleges. This situation is aggravated by a recent trend in theological training which is to encourage students to begin their studies at a first degree level, often coming straight from school. This is disturbing, for such young people devoid of experience of life, and as yet without tertiary education, are unable critically to assess the content of what is taught, and tend to accept and repeat material without fully realising the consequences to their faith. While vaunting open minds, their minds may be simply empty. Those who stand for nothing often fall for anything!

Furthermore the type of training in which a student may engage is far from comprehensive and indeed in places is positively scanty. Despite having attended in excess of the required number of courses for a B.D. I will become a minister of the Word and Sacrament having studied only 2½ books of the New Testament and with hardly a single lecture on the theology of the Sacraments, the Holy Spirit, or even of the Church itself.[1] Yet the General Assembly's regulations say that the courses of study must include homiletics, worship, sacraments, the devotional life etc. Now further New Testament and theology courses are available but only to the exclusion of some other course. If a student's prior contact with Christian doctrine was at a Youth Fellowship level, and if he did not readily turn to private personal reading to make good the gaps, what kind of minister could he possibly be with that type of training? It is recognised that a degree of choice is beneficial, and that in three years a College can only provide a rudimentary education, but the rudiments must still be taught.

While advocating a more positive biblical and theological approach concentrating on the central aspects of Christian doctrine, I would want to make clear that in no way am I suggesting any form of "policing" of staff or student. The time to take care about the quality of teacher and his priorities is at his appointment. Is it unnecessary to suggest that living faith and a love for God's revelation be among the qualifications for those entrusted to equip the next generation of Church leaders? Freedom is essential, but perhaps it must be seen less as a right and more as a responsibility, and the student or staff member must respond to academic freedom in good faith.

To use one of Jesus' illustrations, the Christian thinker must lose his life, his freedom, his academic ambitions in order to find himself precisely as a Christian thinker, be he student or member of staff. It is the discipline of the narrow way which in the end will prove most liberating for the Church and for the World.

I would reject any form of legislation for reform, with its tendency to judgmental attitudes, simple external conformity and consequently a barren, sterile legalistic orthodoxy. But I do long for people with a true faith and bright mind to develop and enhance the leadership of God's Church in Scotland for the future. How this can be done in human terms I do not know, for I fear the Church will always get the Colleges it deserves. A final quote from Professor Torrance: "What has happened? We seem to have allowed a secularisation of ministry to creep in upon us to such an extent that the sense of our consecration together with Christ in the ministry of the Gospel has become dim . . . What we need is a profound and wide-ranging spiritual and evangelical renewal of our people, ministry and congregations alike, until Christ and his Gospel are put in the centre and holiness is recovered as an essential mark of the Church and its ministry." I believe this can only come from God himself and to that end we must work and pray.

NOTE

1. Since autumn 1979 the situation at Edinburgh has been amended, but how many other loopholes still exist in the Scottish Colleges?

9

The case for a Church College

GEORGE T. H. REID

I

It would be surprising if the Church of Scotland were not concerned about the training for its ministry today, for it is this concern that is exciting many different Churches throughout the world. The papers published by the World Council of Churches on "Ministerial Formation" reveal how widespread this interest has become, and it is fascinating to note how many of the reports from geographically widely separated Churches have much the same story to tell.

From Africa we have this: "The question of what kind of education future ministers will need is a major problem . . . The Church has simply not adapted the ministry to the needs of the people, and is too afraid to abandon structures and rules which are suffocating Christian communities."

From North America we have this: "Seminaries [we would call them Theological Colleges] have been so covetous of academic recognition that they have not noticed how alien and hostile that premise is to the peculiar vocation of the Seminary . . . The appropriate location for the Seminary is within the Church, the body of Christ, and not within the University."

From South America we have this: "The training of the new priest required today will not be aimed at producing the classic academic type usual [in the ministry] today, but the sound Christian capable of passing on the Gospel message, engendering faith in those around him."

From South India we have this: "We question if this [the academic training favoured by the West] will help people to take their vocation as Christians seriously, or whether it will not make them slip into the easier task of becoming theological teachers."

Paper 2 on Ministerial Formation sums up the matter like this: "In recent years Theological Colleges have come increasingly under attack, as being irrelevant, cut off from the realities of congregational life, human misery and the social struggles of our time."

Here we might add the comment made by a young Anglican vicar, "I believe the methods of training priests will have to be changed, so that they are taught to communicate the Christian faith effectively . . . They have been trained as though their role was to teach academic theology, rather than be priest, teacher, pastor and leader to a living Christian community faced with the tensions [of modern life]."[1]

The common factor in all these criticisms coming from so many different quarters is the rejection of the academic kind of education for the ministry of which we in the Church of Scotland for long have been so proud. This rejection does not arise from any obscurantism or revolt against the intellect. It arises from wide experience which has exposed the inadequacy of an academic education as a preparation for Christian ministry. It has been tried and found wanting.

We must not underestimate the importance of intellectual discipline. We remember how the Lord saw that it was good to recruit Saul with his degree from the Rabbinical College to supplement the apostolic mission of the "untrained laymen" (Acts 4:13) who were Jesus' first disciples. Among the three main reasons for the triumph of Christianity over the Roman Empire, T.R. Glover notes the fact that "the Christians out-thought the pagan world". In every generation the Church needs men of great intellectual ability to provide the appropriate apologetic for their day.

But an academic education is not sufficient to furnish a Christian mind. It was not a Ph.D. in Old Testament studies that gave Paul his authority, but the power of the Holy Spirit. If he ranks with the intellectual giants of all time, the most distinctive feature of his mind was that it was illuminated and ablaze with the love of God. It is doubtful if such properties would commend themselves to the appointing committee of a University Faculty today. The committee would be more likely to favour the "open-ended" and "non-directive" attitudes which have become such a fetish with modern educationists. Paul was not only a great theologian; primarily he was a "man in Christ". Here lies the true qualification for any Christian teacher whether his role be in the pulpit or the professor's chair.

We have already noted the comment made from the Church of South India, that it is easier to slip into teaching theology than to take seriously the vocation of being a Christian. The secular university cannot be expected to be concerned about this sort of distinction but it is one that any true education for the ministry must take into account. The true function of a Divinity College is not to turn out B.D. graduates, but "sound Christians" as the report from South America already noted has it — "capable of engendering faith in those around them".

When Prof. Hans Kung was asked why, in view of his liberal theology denounced by Rome, he did not declare himself a Protestant he replied: "Protestantism! Ach! Too cerebral!" The criticism is entirely justified and is particularly applicable to the Church of Scotland. We have been very proud of our "educated ministry" and of the intellectual quality of our Church's preaching. But it takes more than cerebration to make a Christian. The true response to God is to love him not with mind alone, but with all our heart and all our soul and all our strength. The disproportionate importance attached by the Church of Scotland to academic values has affected the whole ethos of our Church and is responsible for much of its weakness today.

For one thing it is at least partly responsible for the apparent failure of the Church in communication. It is not only the language used but the kind of thinking that alienates the academically trained from those who have not had a similar education. The Rev. John Lyall, until recently field officer of the Church of Scotland Department on Education, out of his wide travels throughout Scotland reported: "Meeting with several groups of ministers and elders, I discovered that with few exceptions the phraseology of the pulpit bears little relevance to the man in the pew. As one elder puts it: 'The minister is trained in an intellectual arena which is foreign to the vast majority of his hearers'." I believe that this is one of the main reasons why the Church of Scotland has become disproportionately middle-class, and functions most successfully in well-to-do suburban areas where there is a high level of education. But it is to the poor that we are first commissioned to preach the Gospel. We would do well to ponder the criticism already quoted that theological institutions tend to cut their students off "from the realities of congregational life, human misery, and the social struggles of our time".

But by far the most serious consequence of the undue academic bias of our present education for the ministry is the truly astonishing degree to which spirituality has been ignored. A ray of hope can be seen in the recent shift in emphasis by the Department of Practical Theology at Edinburgh to include a course on prayer for the first time! This of course is a gap which reflects the weakness of the whole Church, and should not be blamed on the Colleges alone. In its 1979 Report, the Committee on Education for the Ministry notes that previous attempts to provide retreats organised "from above" were unsuccessful, but welcomes the greater interest now being shown by students themselves in spirituality. But to refer to "teaching on prayer and spirituality . . . in the Colleges" as if it was a significant part of the curriculum is to mislead the Church as to what really goes on in Divinity Faculties.

When Angelo Roncalli, now known as the late Pope John XXIII, was a student in the Seminary at Bergamo, he and other fellow-students were offered "The Little Rules" prescribing a rigorous discipline for the spiritual life, which Angelo Roncalli sought to obey all his days. The aim of the Little Rules was "to provide a way of life for the seminarist who wishes to advance on the way to perfection". The reference to a Roman Catholic Seminary will I fear be sufficient to alienate the bigoted, and may lead others to imagine that I am advocating the monastic type of spirituality practised by the Church of Rome. I mean nothing of the kind, but use the reference to ask: are our Divinity Colleges at all concerned about helping our students along the way to perfection, and if they are, what actual assistance are they giving for this end? (If you shy at the word "perfection", then read "the true fulfilment of our Christian calling".) Again I note that in his short addresses to novitiates, Cardinal Basil Hume urges: "The important thing in the novitiate is that you should learn to become men of prayer, learn the art of prayer, learn the practice of the presence of God: that you should become men of God."[2] Again I make reference to a Roman Catholic institution to ask if in our Divinity Colleges there is any comparable importance attached to learning the art of prayer, and the practice of the presence of God. Would I be wholly wrong in suggesting that the main concern in our Divinity Colleges is geared to turning out, not men of God, but Batchelors of Divinity?

When fifty years ago much the same question was put to Baron von Hugel as was addressed to Hans Kung, "Why do you not leave the Church of Rome?", he answered, "Because I cannot find elsewhere the same degree of sanctity". Together with the majority of our Church of Scotland members, I believe that the Church of Rome is in error; and that even their idea of sanctity is at fault. But is not the error of the Church of Scotland even greater in that as our own Prof. John Baillie confessed: "We have allowed the idea of sanctity to grow dim, the desire for it to become abnormal." We are all "called to be saints" and the Church or the individual who has forgotten, or given up striving, to fulfil this calling has forfeited the right to be called Christian. This grave fault is woven into the system of our education for the ministry. Would I be wrong to suggest that in our Divinity Colleges the main concern is not that our students should grow in love and humility and obedience, the marks of sanctity? The main concern is that they should acquire sufficient marks to pass their degree exams.

When I received my July "Life and Work", as I was writing this chapter, I was especially interested to note that Mr. Kernohan had entitled a very powerful article by Prof. Tom Torrance, "A serious call for a return to devout and holy life", for it had already been my intention to refer here to William Law's book, which made such an extraordinary impact on his day, and profoundly affected such various men as John Wesley, Samuel Johnson, and John Keble. Yet the essential message of the book is very simple. It is that the ineffectiveness, the mediocrity and tepidity of the Christianity of the times, despite its regular church-going, was due to nothing else than the lack of any serious intention to marry profession and practice. "If you will here ask yourself why you are not as pious as the primitive Christians were, your own heart will tell you, that it is neither through ignorance or inability but purely because you never thoroughly intended it." Is this not the radical fault of the Church of Scotland today and is it not reflected in the nature of the education given for its ministry? Is the first serious intention of our Divinity Colleges to train faithful servants of Jesus? Or have they not become distracted from any such intention through their preoccupation with academic interests?

II

So now the question arises: can the Divinity Colleges, now merged with the secular Universities where academic values have first priority, be expected to provide the new education for the ministry in which spiritual values are given first place? Frankly I do not think they can. This does not imply any criticism of the Universities who apparently have leant backwards in order to accommodate themselves to the peculiar needs of ministerial formation. The fact is however that the values of the secular University are different from the values which Divinity Colleges should hold, and it would be unfair to expect Universities to be other than true to themselves. We should respect one another's differences, but we must also be true to our values.

Since the Colleges became merged with the Universities some twenty years ago there have been new difficulties. The Church of Scotland has no longer independent control over the appointments made to lectureships and chairs in our Colleges. In the Divinity classes now, a large proportion of the students have no intention of entering the Church of Scotland or any other ministry. This makes pastoral care and attention to the special needs of candidates for the ministry difficult. These difficulties were entirely predictable and they may well become more acute in the future despite the goodwill shown by Universities at present.

The function of a Church College however would not be in my view to provide a rival theological centre, but rather to provide the necessary supplement to practical training, which in our Colleges has rarely if ever been satisfactory, and to spirituality which has been virtually ignored. By this I do not mean an in-turned pietistic ghetto or a hot house for artificially forced spirituality. I mean a College which will provide an additional kind of training which the University cannot and perhaps should not be expected to give.

I have no talent for organisation and may well run into absurdities when I attempt to suggest a rough outline for such training. If I do, I hope these absurdities will not prejudice the reader against the idea of a Church College more sensibly planned. For what it is worth I envisage a College which all candidates for the ministry will attend in their probationary year. The difficulty of bringing them together will be great but not insurmountable and I believe worth while overcoming. The practical training here would be given by parish ministers of proved effectiveness enlisted on a part-time short-term basis. They would come from areas representing a wide variety of ministry. Lectures would be given on parish ministry and on spirituality during the morning, while in the evenings and afternoons, students would serve in the parishes to which they were allotted or in missions, so that teaching and practice could go hand in hand to the mutual advantage of both. Formerly divinity students were able to receive appointment as assistants in various churches during their College training. The practice has been discontinued on the grounds that such practical work should not be allowed to interfere with students' studies, and replaced with "attachments". Here again the academic bias of Church of Scotland training is showing, and suggests the folly of the apocryphal Japanese head master who, on hearing that the British empire was won on the playing fields of Eton, imported booklets containing the rules of cricket making these required reading for his pupils, and set an examination on them at the end of the year without offering them the least opportunity for actually playing the game. The emphasis the Church of South India attaches to meshing the study of theology with missionary activity as the only means of truly learning theology is worth noting here. Time in College would be allowed for discussion in which students would air, and be given guidance for, the problems encountered in their practical work and spiritual growth.

About three years ago a speaker asked the General Assembly to consider making St. Colms into an Ecumenical College of Divinity. At the Assembly this year I asked the Committee on Education for the Ministry to consider the use of St. Colms for a Church College, as I thought the cost of building or acquiring new premises would be beyond our means. There are of course other properties belonging to the Church — Carberry Tower, St. Ninians and Iona Abbey. I made special mention of St. Colms for though the present accommodation is largely already taken up, I am assured the grounds about the house are sufficient to provide room for the building of annexes, and moreover there are three good reasons that make St. Colms especially suitable.

1   The declared policy of St. Colms is "to offer a training within a community of faith and so the residential nature of the College and the importance given to worship and the devotional experience are at the heart of all else". This is precisely the kind of fellowship the secular University cannot be expected to provide,

but which every candidate for the ministry should have the opportunity of experiencing for some part of his training.

2   In St. Colms, candidates for the ministry would meet with those training for overseas and home mission, and as deacons. The W.C.C. papers on "Ministerial Formation" speak of a certain "elitism" in the Church. Ministers are often regarded within the Church, and perhaps are even prone to regard themselves, as the officer class; home missionaries and deaconesses, even overseas missionaries, are regarded as belonging to the N.C.O. class or other ranks. It might be hoped that through living together all at St. Colms might come to a fuller understanding of their respective roles, and to appreciate that all service is uniquely valued by God, and there is no first or last. That such new understanding is necessary is indicated by the all too frequent complaint of deaconesses, that many ministers have no idea as to how best deaconesses should be used.

3   St. Colms has always stressed the importance of personal relationships, which provide the ground for the practice of Christianity. Ministers are prone to become individualists. The witness of collegiate charges, team ministries, College staff rooms, is too often wretchedly disabled by the inability of ministers to work harmoniously together. What is really at fault here is a failure in that kind of loving by which Jesus warned us men might know that we are Christians. I do not know if in our Divinity Colleges the least attention is being paid to helping candidates for the ministry to grow in such love. I do know there is no more important matter related to our growth as Christians, and that it is one which in view of the likely development of team ministries will become increasingly important. St. Colms has for long sought to promote the practice of Christian relationships.

The idea of an independent Church College of course is no new one. Every other major denomination in Scotland except the Church of Scotland has one for their ministerial formation. In the Church of Scotland Lord George MacLeod with accustomed percipience was advocating such a college twenty years ago.[3] Many ministers since then have expressed the same view. The Wolfe Report at this year's General Assembly speaks of "the possible tension between University and Church requirements" and suggests the possibility of a Church College. But in the general consideration of the Wolfe Report,[4] we read that the Committee on Education for the Ministry has "roundly excluded the suggestion from their concern within the past year". I hope the Committee may give it serious consideration in the coming year. It is my belief that the exigencies of the situation are such as to make the establishment of some sort of Church College sooner or later inevitable. The sooner the cheaper; the sooner the better.

NOTES

1. Michael Wright, *New Ways for Christ*
2. Basil Hume, *Searching for God* p.38
3. George MacLeod, *One Way Left* pp.95-96
4. Church of Scotland *1979 Assembly Reports* p.497
5. Part of this Appendix was printed as a letter in the September 1979 edition of *Life and Work*, and is reproduced with permission.

Appendix

ROBERT A. JONES

Starting a Church College with State grants to students might involve sacrificing the aid at present received by candidates for the "vocational" part of their present training, e.g. for the two year Diploma in Pastoral Studies. The following assumes that after careful negotiation, the Church received grants for the Church College year and that the grant aided period at University was in some cases reduced by one (or two) years.

The Church of Scotland could then expect to receive the same fees at present charged by the Universities, and normally paid by the government. With about sixty students in training per year, and fees running at over £600, that could provide an annual income for a College of about £36,000.

If the Church were to run its own educational establishment, it would probably coordinate within it the facilities now provided at St. Colms College and Carberry Tower. The operating expenditure at St. Colms and the deficit at Carberry Tower would then also be available to swell the College purse.

1. Thus, the estimate of the possibilities of finance available for a one year Church College could be as follows:

Students' fees at current University level
    60 students at £632   37,920

Operating Expenditure of St. Colms College
    in 1978   61,150

Payment by Parish Education Committee
    to meet deficit at Carberry Tower
    — 1978   __24,500__
                                    £123,570

2. If it was desired to provide a full three year Church College, and let students get what University education they could previously (somewhat as the Roman Catholics do, with State aid) then the picture could be as follows:

Student fees, 180 at £632	113,760
Payment to Divinity Colleges by Education for Ministry Committee, 1978	30,700
Operating expenditure of St. Colms, 1978	61,150
Payment to meet Carberry deficit, 1978	24,500
	£230,110

The writer has no idea whether such a sum would allow a Church College to be viable, but two points can be made:

(a) The committee of Forty Report of 1977, Section VII, 1(3) contained the following statement: "The Wolfe Report estimated the cost of maintaining a Church College to be in the region of £160,000".

(b) Until a full investigation is carried out, with more detailed facts and figures available, no one can write off the possibility of the Church educating its own students for the ministry on financial grounds alone.

10
What now?

JOCK STEIN

I

The present system of training ministers relies on a partnership between Church and University. The Church, through its Committee on Education for the Ministry, is responsible for training ministers, and the University, through the Faculty of Divinity, for educating them. The two liaise at various points, in particular the Board of Practical Training and the four Departments of Practical Theology.

Two developments have occurred since mid-century which have placed a strain upon this partnership:

1. The introduction of the B.D. as a first degree has meant that a good proportion of divinity students start their theological education straight after school, or at least in their late teens. Previously, men arrived with another degree (often in philosophy from a Scottish university) or other experience (maybe war service), and were mature enough to study divinity as further education and vocational training combined.

   The higher proportion of younger men and women today has meant that the accent falls on education rather than training. One of the reasons why the Faculties introduced the "first B.D." was that for a time many candidates could not get into Arts before doing Divinity. Another was to attract more younger people to read theology. Success here has meant that the proportion of candidates for the Church of Scotland ministry is low (at St Andrews, as low as 10%).

H

It is not a bad thing in itself for young people to study theology as part of their life exploration. Again, others considering the possibility of ordination may study divinity for a time before being officially accepted as candidates for the ministry. The selection schools are wisely cautious of accepting too young a candidate. But this trend does mean that the character and outlook of the student body has changed, and that many more students themselves do not see their education as just one side of training for service in the Church.

2. The growing specialisation of theology, in common with other disciplines, has meant that fewer and fewer staff with experience of the parish ministry have been appointed to College posts. To keep up academically, it is considered necessary to continue research and teaching, full time. Also, readjustment has reduced the number of "quiet" parishes where a minister can devote considerable time to academic study before returning to a teaching post.

In a Church Seminary, you would expect four criteria to be considered in making appointments:

1. Quality of spiritual life and commitment to Jesus Christ
2. Academic qualifications
3. Teaching ability
4. Experience of the life and work of the Church in question.

In staff appointments to Divinity Faculties, the second of these by far outweighs the others, if in fact the other three are considered at all. It is of course well known that Faculties in general appoint many staff who are bad at teaching but good at research and writing — but why must this also be true of Faculties of Divinity? (And why, incidentally, do some men who are compelling preachers make such dull lecturers!)

In fact, one Faculty does put the Divinity Faculty to shame. It is not uncommon for a Professor of Clinical Medicine to say, "I could not continue teaching students if I was not involved in the practice of medicine!" Now of course it was at one time a scandal that a Professor of Divinity might have a parish charge which he neglected — which is why "pluralism" (the word in those days) was given up. But many city ministers would welcome having members of the Departments of Practical Theology working in a team ministry with them!

Sadly, the reason why Divinity falls behind Medicine may be simply that our society takes very seriously bodily disorders, and so the teaching of medicine as a practical science is taken equally seriously. We do not as a society take spiritual disorders seriously, or rather it is fashionable to reduce them all to medical and psychological problems. Even Departments of Practical Theology are prone to lay stress on the importance of psychology and sociology in pastoral counselling at the expense of prayer, spiritual diagnosis and application of Christian doctrine.

One more hopeful sign is that hospital chaplains can hold university teaching posts — but parish ministers very seldom do, and here it may be the Church which is at fault, failing to react flexibly to new circumstances.

All this again means that education and training fall apart, as the relation of education to parish life and work means less to the college staff. Departments of P.T. try to compensate for this by inviting parish ministers to lecture, or by "attaching" students to parishes, as required by the Committee on Education for the Ministry. These procedures are useful, but unfortunately throw the gap between the full time academic staff and the parish into sharper relief.

II

However the partnership itself is coming under attack from two very different angles. Readers may be inclined to identify with one or the other, but both argue that the present *concordat* is detrimental in practice to the witness of the Church of Scotland. The previous chapter drew on both of them in seeking to go further and argue that Church and University have in principle different values; but it may be useful at this stage to distinguish the two angles, because they represent on the whole different groups in the Church.

The *first* angle views critically the divergence from Church orthodoxy on the part of some Divinity teaching staff. This is not of course a new complaint. What is new is that some such critics are no longer prepared to "thole" the system in the hope that getting more orthodox people appointed to chairs and lectureships would automatically put things right.

The growth of new attitudes to biblical criticism, and the weakening of calvinist orthodoxy, began last century or earlier. Nevertheless, whatever may have been the case elsewhere, in Scotland theological teachers who may have disagreed in their attitudes to scripture, predestination, evolution, churchmanship, stood together on the basic Christian doctrines of Incarnation and Resurrection. In fact it has been one of the strengths of Scottish theological education that Colleges did not divide as in England into camps of "high", "broad" and "evangelical".

It is historically dangerous to suggest that in one's own day the bastions of Christian doctrine have at last begun to fall. There have been "heretics" in every generation. One hundred years after McLeod Campbell was deposed for heresy he was praised in a centennial eulogy by no less a person than the Principal of New College. Nevertheless, theologians and ministers exercise a freedom to "reinterpret" doctrines like the Resurrection which would have been called unbelief fifty years ago. It is a fair criticism that the Kirk has gone into beliefs on Baptism with a toothcomb and conveniently ignored far bigger deviations from Presbyterian orthodoxy. Sooner or later the Church of Scotland must move beyond the "escape clause" to the Westminster Confession, and formulate afresh the "substance of the Faith".

You may think this is good academic freedom. What is certainly true is that it increases the tension between Church and University. If, as sometimes happens, Divinity students label certain lecturers as "non-Christians" or "unsound in doctrine", this will hardly help the preparation of these students for the ministry, whatever you think of the impact of such teaching on the other students who lap it up eagerly.

On a recent TV panel it was argued that the Kirk's interests were safeguarded because the Committee on Education for the Ministry sets the courses which candidates for the ministry must cover. But this is facile. Even if it is true — and chapter 8 illustrates the loopholes — what matters just as much is who teaches the course, what he or she believes, how he approaches the subject, how well or badly he communicates, how effectively he enables learning to take place. To take the first point, belief, it makes a vast difference whether the Resurrection is presented as a myth which "gives meaning to life", or as an event in history which gives hope now and in the life to come. When someone is dying it is one thing to say, "The early Christians believed in the

Jesus myth and so can you"; quite another to say in the words of the New Testament, "Because Jesus lives, we shall live also."

The *second* angle is also congruent with the growing attention paid to the Bible in recent decades, but is a criticism "from below" rather than "from above". Biblical studies have focused more sharply of late on God's love for the poor and for those outside the "establishment" of the age. There is a suspicion that the pride which the Kirk has taken in having an educated ministry just might be the wrong kind of pride. It is put very bluntly by Carlos Christo in a letter to a friend; he writes from prison where he awaits trial because he has helped a fugitive:

> "You mentioned how difficult it is to establish a dialogue with the poor because their language is nearly incomprehensible to the cleric. The difficulty is of our own making. We have dissociated ourselves from the normal concerns of most people's lives under the pretext of thus becoming available for preaching the gospel . . . Our classical education alters our way of thinking and our vocabulary. The long training period in the cloister removes us from the real problems that affect the lives of everyone except the clergy and the rich."[1]

Carlos is writing of course about the Roman Catholic Church in Brazil, some distance indeed away from the Kirk. But if you visit some of the vast Scottish housing estates where the poor and unemployed are concentrated, you will find similar attitudes expressed about the Kirk as were expressed by the poor of Latin America a decade ago about "their" church. Mind you, I could prove them wrong in part, at least to my own satisfaction (how different Scotland is, after all etc). But would they believe me? And if the Gospel is not being communicated clearly by the words and actions of the Church, then how can Jesus Christ be satisfied?

There is much to be said for having Theological Colleges part of a University. Above all perhaps, it applies the Gospel: theology and theological education can be seen as pursued not just for the Church, but for the World. But here comes the catch. For whose world? The world of the poor and disadvantaged . . . or the world of the suburbs and the Scotsman? Could it be that in our Colleges today, students fall between two stools — they are no longer part of the workaday world of the majority of citizens, but neither are they part of a Christian community seriously training *as a body* for Christian discipleship.

So run the two arguments. It may be useful to spell out why they are controversial. The controversy stems from the presuppositions, as well as some dispute over the facts of the analysis. (For example, at a conference for ministers working in church extension areas, ministers from Glasgow argued strongly along the line taken by Carlos Christo; ministers from Dundee argued that the community was not divided and that ordinary people were not so alienated from the Kirk. Did this reflect a difference in presuppositions, or just that Dundee as a whole is largely a one-class area?)

The first argument presented above against the partnership, or *concordat*, presupposes a body of orthodox Christian doctrine, maybe growing in sophistication with its interpretation over the centuries but still recognisably "the Faith once delivered to the saints". Its proponents are sometimes called theologically "conservative". And with some notable exceptions those who are conservative in theology tend to be conservative also in politics.

The second argument presupposes a traditional marxist analysis of society into classes, the bourgeois rich versus the proletarian poor. Its proponents are (in the West!) called politically "radical". And again with some notable exceptions those who are radical in politics tend to be radical also in theology (if they believe at all).

Yet an alliance (holy or unholy) might emerge between theological conservatives and radicals who agree that the present system is defective, and who might both desire a Church College where the true faith could be taught and lived. The alliance would come under great pressure when it came to making appointments, planning courses and establishing the ethos of the College. But it is not unthinkable. One of the reassuring and challenging points to emerge from overseas countries undergoing violent social change is this: when the chips are down, and Christians have to stand up and be counted, radical and conservative may be found shoulder to shoulder when the compromisers have all left the arena.

Such a confrontation might on the other hand be immensely beneficial if it could become a dialogue with mutual trust. There is more such dialogue going on outside Scotland than inside.[2] It depends in part on the emergence of more figures like the late Kenneth Mackenzie, who was politically radical and theologically conservative.

In any event, a Church College could only succeed if it were part of a positive strategy by the Church, and not simply a negative reaction against "theological wreckers" in the University; just as a federal or independent Scotland could only be successful as part of a Scottish psychological and cultural renaissance, not as an anti-English reaction.

In 1871 A.B. Bruce published the first edition of his famous book, *The Training of the Twelve*. There the experience of the first disciples with Jesus is presented as a model for minister and members alike. Now the Church of Scotland has chosen to see Saul of Tarsus with his higher education as the norm, and not Peter the fisherman. But Saul required a new kind of education after his conversion, and in any case (as chapter 9 argues) can we any longer take him as the norm? There was a time when higher education in Scotland took place within what was at least assumed to be a Christian world-view (the time when the atheism of David Hume precluded him from a chair); there was a time when University education was the dream of every lad o' pairts, and when Government policy was to expand University places; but none of these are true today. We may still need an elite, as Bishop Newbigin points out, but this should no longer, on biblical or sociological grounds, be the sole or even the normal pattern for preparing Church leaders for service.

It is not that we want an uneducated ministry! But are our ministers educated in the school of Christ? The traditional distinction between education (University) and training (Church) may be misleading in principle anyway, because Christian education is not simply acquiring knowledge, nor just personal development, but a deliberate process of learning with a view to change in character — indoctrination in the proper, not the pejorative sense. The word sometimes used is "formation", and it was because of a wish to stress formation rather than education that St. Colm's College developed its own courses independently of Edinburgh University in the 1970s.

There are really only three ways forward:

1. To improve the present system, which means that the Committee on Education for the Ministry must continue to close the loopholes in approved courses, and that the Church exercise more discrimination in those appointments in which it has a say — as it has every legal and moral right to do.

2. To opt out of the system and set up a Church College as an alternative to University education. It might come to this, and the Committee on Education for the Ministry should cease being shocked by the suggestion, and start keeping the implications under review.

3. To recognise that it will be problematic, even if not impossible, to hold together education and training in a University setting, and therefore to pursue complementary alternatives, so that the Church gets as far as possible the best of both worlds — or to use a happier and more biblical expression, like the Church legal expert trained for the Kingdom it makes use of both the old and the new. This is the approach I wish to illustrate in conclusion, although less dramatically than chapter 9.

III

The life of the apostles had three parts:
1. Home and synagogue education, and prior experience of life.
2. Learning in word and action with Jesus — what today might be called praxis.
3. Subsequent service with Jesus present by his Spirit.

As we might hope with such a model, in God's wisdom it divides theologically into three categories — the providence of God the Father in their background, the purpose of God the incarnate Son in their three years training, the presence of God the Spirit in their later ministry (in which of course their learning continued).

It would be nice to think that the model sheds light as follows on our training for the ministry:
1. Upbringing and formal education, initial sense of "the call".
2. Three years or more at College, supplemented by a probationary year.
3. Ordination and subsequent service.

I suspect that most Church members, if they give any thought to it, would regard time spent at Theological College as training for service, i.e. the second period above. But I trust this book has indicated how superficial that view is; nor would it be held *simpliciter* by teaching staff.

Time spent at a University Faculty of Divinity cannot clearly be seen as life and learning with Jesus. Suppose instead that we regard it as part of the first section, so that we neither devalue it altogether nor regard it as central to training for the ministry. This would run parallel to the concern of chapter 4 that the Divinity Colleges should be used for the education of lay leaders as well as ordained. (And now that St. Colm's College has made its point about "formation", not just "education", it might wish to make use afresh of one or two courses at New College without fearing domination.)

Before we look more positively at the training section, let us bring another consideration into focus. Jesus himself was about thirty when he was called to preach in public; he chose working men, including the married; and the local leaders of the early Christian churches were called "elders". The exception, Timothy, was liable to encounter opposition in his ministry because of his youth, we are told.

We should be a little suspicious of the school — Theological College — ordination pattern, even with a diploma in pastoral studies and a probationary year in the middle. An overseas Presbyterian Church Assembly resolved that no one should be admitted to Theological College unless they had spent a year out of school and involved in the life of a local church. It is not a big step to suggesting that the norm, not the exception, should be that ordained ministers are chosen from among those who have already proved themselves as leaders in the local church, even if this means (surprise!) that they are as old as thirty. If this results in fewer ordained ministers for a while, that might encourage us further to take lay leadership seriously, and to give younger people experience of leadership.

Training therefore in this context is not just something that a committee lays on from outside — it is a process continuing in the life of the local church; for many, perhaps the majority, training for the ministry of Word and Sacrament will begin long before they study divinity at a College; in fact, methods of theological education by extension may prove better for some than prolonged residential study.

However the Church of Scotland is not yet as ready to change in the light of New Testament norms as overseas Presbyterian Churches. So we come now to look at the present situation, and in particular the "probationary year", since this is the period most open to immediate constructive change.

Any rough survey of opinion among probationers reveals two things. First, that most probationers see this as the time when they really learn what the ministry is all about. Second, that "bishops" (nickname for the ministers who oversee probationers) vary from very effective to very poor as trainers. Nor is the latter surprising when you remember that probationers are allocated (a) to churches which can afford to pay them, (b) to churches which are given a grant by the Home Board for an assistant minister — not necessarily to churches with the skills and the setting in which best to train the probationer. It is true that probationers are invited later to comment on the effectiveness of their bishops; but this makes little difference; I know of one case where two very different probationers gave one senior church statesman an appalling report two years running, but probationers are still happily or unhappily being allocated to him.

IV

The following proposal would not necessarily be endorsed by the other contributors to this book, but it is consistent with the various points made and could be done without much upheaval. It involves three changes of principle.

1. Congregations should no longer be allowed a probationer simply because they can afford to pay one (or get a grant to do so).
2. Under the Board of Education (or whatever), there should be a single committee to oversee both the education and the training of ministers from start to finish, and not two committees as at present.
3. The primary purpose of the probationary year should become the training of the probationer, not as at present the filling of a post.

The first change does not mean that a demanding church and parish has to do without a second fulltime church worker! In some cases it would be better for a congregation to have an assistant minister for three or four years, than a probationer who is always moving on after one or two years. With the amalgamation of congregations there is rightly or wrongly less scope for the minister who is not ready to jump straight from his probationary year into a fairly big charge, or for the older minister who wants to "retire" to a small charge. The Kirk would benefit if more older men finished as associate ministers, perhaps part time.

Nor is it essential for the assistant to be ordained. If the senior minister is primarily wanting help with weddings and baptisms, he needs an ordained man or woman; though in Scotland the current decline of folk religion coupled with the slow tightening of standards in the Church will mean a fairly dramatic decline in the number of church marriages and infant baptisms over the next decade. But in many situations a trained layman would be as effective; Scotland is slow to move here, the best example is probably St. Aldate's Church in Oxford, where a former war time pilot who used to head up the English Inter-Schools Christian Fellowship now works in partnership with Michael Green, rector of the main city church; Branse Burbridge his associate has special responsibility for city centre chaplaincy work and lunch time services.

The second change was well argued by James Miller in the August 1979 copy of Life and Work. It is significant that some presbyteries like Dundee already have only one committee to cover education and training — known as the Students and Probationers Committee. The new single committee should incidentally have the four College Principals on it; the Principal of a College (a Church appointment) is responsible for the pastoral oversight of candidates for the ministry while they are at College; and for the way in which training relates and is seen to relate to education during the course, which is one reason why the office is often combined with that of Dean of Faculty — but it may be sometimes more helpful to the Church for different people to hold the two posts, as also happens.

The third change would allow training to be modelled a little more closely on the first disciples' praxis with Jesus. In a number of Presbyteries, including certainly the four in the large cities, a key minister would be chosen to oversee a group of probationers, and together they would function as a "college" for a year. The probationers would be placed in various parishes, but would meet together for say one day each week of analysis, study and prayer with their (common) bishop. Let us tease out the various strands of this proposal.

The overseeing minister, or *director*, need not as at present be someone with a big charge, overburdened and anxious to shed work. He might well be an older minister working part time in a city charge. The principle of selecting one person like this is not unpresbyterian, because we already have conveners responsible to Presbytery for different tasks. He would need to be a person who combined spirituality with skills as a director of training, and at the same time someone acceptable to young (and critical!) probationers of different outlooks.

The *probationers* would need accommodation and salary. The cheaper, but less beneficial, way would be for probationers to be allocated largely as at present, so that they are paid by the congregations where they are placed, who get five rather than six days work a week from them. (As the alternative would be to employ an ordained assistant, or a layman, both of whom would cost more than a probationer, even the more mercenary congregations would still be likely to accept probationers under the new terms.) Better would be the provision of some central funding so that some probationers could be attached to congregations which in themselves could not justify an extra minister financially, but where training opportunities abound (as is done in a somewhat perfunctory way with students attached from College.)

Probationers could live in houses supplied by the parish of their placement as at present, but congregations, realising that probationers were no longer "guaranteed" to them might not wish to retain such accommodation; in such cases council houses could be rented on a Presbytery basis, or a redundant manse used for single probationers.

They would be responsible to the minister and Kirk Session of their parish for any work done there, but to their director overall; just as during College at present a student can be attached to a parish but still remain under the Department of Practical Theology. If confidence in the scheme grew so that central funding increased, they could be placed in pairs in key missionary situations, and also gain extra experience of industrial and other chaplaincy work.

The *local minister* with whom probationers were associated would no longer be their bishop. But he or she could helpfully be involved by the director in the life of the "college". Each would discuss carefully with the director the aim and practice of training beforehand, and the director would liaise on behalf of *Presbytery* with the new *Committee on Education and Training*. It would be possible for the director to be also convener of the local committee, or the Presbytery might prefer another to undertake this.

It might be possible for the director to cooperate with other denominations. The three big challenges in Scotland are relationships with Roman Catholics, Baptists and the Free Kirk. The situation varies markedly from place to place, but ministers and priests hold the key to progress in this area, assuming that Presbyteries and bishops do not forbid it. Dialogue at high levels is not achieving major breakthroughs, and common social action has proved useful but frustrating in the absence of opportunities for deeper fellowship, prayer and study together. At present divinity students have the chance of exchanges with Roman seminaries; it would be a step forward if this kind of contact was maintained at probationer stage. But this is incidental to the main point.

The "college" would also be a natural focus for youngsters interested in the ministry as a vocation, more effective and appropriate than churchmen touting the holy ministry round schools. In fact the local "college" has immense possibilites beyond its immediate object of training probationers.

Behind this particular suggestion, which might need much emendation in practice, lies a desire to maintain the balance of Christ's life with his disciples; a balance of work and worship, study and withdrawal, the interrelation of theory and practice, action and reflection on it which is summarised by the word "praxis". To use a picture from the gospels, the life of the disciple oscillates between the Mount of Transfiguration and the valley where problems abound.[3] By contrast, the life of a divinity student may so easily contour around a misty slope, neither in touch with God, man or beast.

Another desire is to introduce change by degrees, taking one's cue from the yeast which in time affects the whole dough. The above proposal means in effect mini-Church Colleges, using college in the dynamic rather than the static sense, and would allow the bigger idea of a Church College to be practically assessed and built up in stages if wanted. On the other hand, it would not be the thin end of the wedge, as it would not at all commit the Church of Scotland to withdrawal from the Universities. In fact there is no reason why Divinity teaching staff and other resource people should not also be drawn into the life of the probationers' "college".

V

There is probably at present no clear agreement on the future of training for the ordained ministry. That is partly because underneath the subjects considered in this book lie four issues which the Church of Scotland has not really begun to wrestle with in our generation.

1. *What kind of leadership does the Spirit give to the Church?* In theory we share leadership between ministers and elders. But in practice . . .? May we not be getting the worst of two worlds — priest-ridden in the parish and committee-ridden in the wider sphere?

2. *What kind of doctrine does the Spirit give to the Church?* Do we accept the traditional doctrine of Christ as true man and true God, and use that as a key to unravel other doctrinal issues? Or do we accept it as one model among others in a pluralistic age? And what are the "fundamental doctrines of the Faith"?

3. *What kind of life does the Spirit give to the Church?* How highly do we rate holiness, compared with academic prowess? Why do so many ministers wear academic hoods in the pulpit? What does God do in and through Christians meeting together? What part do the congregation play in worship?

4. *What kind of freedom does the Spirit give to the Church?* The Church in Eastern Europe thrives under most Communist regimes, to the surprise of many of us. Its leaders generally regard the pact between Church and State under Constantine as an act of betrayal. In the next century, will it be right or even possible to continue as an established Church?

In chaper 1, the ministry of Christ was taken as the basis of Christian ministry today. The four questions here emphasise the work of the Spirit. But there is no conflict; Christian theology and practice must move in the dynamic of the Trinity. And even Karl Barth admitted that he could have started his Church Dogmatics from Pentecost!

All over the world, Christianity is in ferment. To return to Scotland is for observers of the Christian scene like moving over from the cooker towards the freezer, in spite of "Reappraisal". The reasons for this lie beyond the scope of this book, and touch on politics and social psychology as well as the history of the Church in Scotland. In general three attitudes (not mutually exclusive) are shown to our situation:

(a) Leave it to God — he will revive the Church in his own good time.

(b) Get on with preaching, praying, witnessing, serving more urgently.

(c) Reform the structures of the Church.

Improving training for the ministry is usually seen in the context of the third. The last two chapters have been largely taken up with analysis and suggestions for reform. But the aim of the whole book is not to present any one change as a panacea for ministerial formation, but to plead that the issues be worked out afresh in the light of Christian theology and principle, not just practice and procedure.

NOTES

1. Carlos Christo, *Letters from a Prisoner of Conscience* p.114. A similar concern was expressed by the Asian Theological Conference meeting in Sri Lanka in January 1979.
2. For example, *Christian Faith and Political Hopes*, published as a reply to the quietist theology of E.R. Norman, includes both conservative and radical theologians. cf also *Towards a Theology of Politics*, by Haddon Willmer (published by the Shaftesbury Project).
3. Bruce Reed, *The Dynamics of Religion* is a fascinating study of religion in society as "oscillation".